ONE
LONG
RIVER
OF SONG

Grace Notes

Saints Passionate and Peculiar

The Grail

The Wet Engine

Spirited Men

Leaping

Credo

Two Voices (with Jim Doyle)

AS EDITOR

The Best Catholic Writing

A Sense of Wonder

God Is Love

Hoʻolauleʻa (with Mahealani Perez-Wendt)

ONE
LONG
RIVER
OF SONG

Notes on Wonder

BRIAN DOYLE

FOREWORD BY DAVID JAMES DUNCAN

Little, Brown and Company
New York Boston London

Little, Brown and Company
Hachette Book Group
1290 Avenue of the Americas, New York, NY 10104
littlebrown.com

First Edition: December 2019

Little, Brown and Company is a division of Hachette Book Group, Inc. The Little, Brown name and logo are trademarks of Hachette Book Group, Inc.

The publisher is not responsible for websites (or their content) that are not owned by the publisher.

Copyright acknowledgments are on pages 247–250.

The Hachette Speakers Bureau provides a wide range of authors for speaking events. To find out more, go to hachettespeakersbureau.com or call (866) 376-6591.

ISBN 978-0-316-49289-8
LCCN 2019938833

10 9 8 7 6 5 4 3 2 1

LSC-C

Printed in the United States of America

*To the overlooked and misunderstood, to
compassion and grace that conquer all division.
To imagination and creativity. May they flow
fearlessly and endlessly.*

Contents

Contents

III.

We Can Take Off Our Masks, or, If We Can't Do That, We Can Squawk Through the Holes in Them. A Squawk Is Better Than Nothing

IV.

This Blistering Perfect Terrible World

Contents

V.

We Are Better Than We Think

VI.

I Walked Out So Full of Hope I'm Sure I Spilled Some by the Door

Contents

Foreword

"A Mystical Project Born of Joy and Desperation"

My great friend Brian Doyle—"BD" to me for a quarter century, so pardon my addiction to calling him that still—was always an unusually fast and proficient writer. But from the 2010 publication of his first novel, *Mink River,* until his fatal brain-tumor diagnosis late in 2016, he caught fire. During that period he published two collections of short stories, four collections of the prose/poem hybrids he dubbed "proems," seven collections of the power-packed short memoirs, epiphanies, and reflections he too reductively called simply "essays," and five more novels. Over the same span he edited *Portland* magazine, under BD's tenure the most heavily awarded alumni magazine in the country as he helped resurrect, for Americans, the ancient and invaluable genre we now call "spiritual writing." It strains my sense of the possible to add that BD was simultaneously giving public readings and talks by the dozens, writing recommendation letters, visiting grade schools, high schools, colleges, and book groups to regale what amounted to thousands of people of all ages, writing rivers of the more entertaining emails on the planet, and privately mentoring, entertaining, and consoling more people than we will ever know. Like any good man or woman dedicated to compassion in a post-fact, post-democratic corporate state, he also kept busy annoying the hell out of a few worthy enemies. I can't resist adding that the typing portion of all these achievements was accomplished with precisely two fingers. I challenge the world's pianists to see what they can do with the same two fingers.

Brian's nonfiction appeared in scores of America's finest magazines, won three Pushcart Prizes, and was regularly reprinted in every major nonfiction anthology in the country—including seven times in *Best American Essays*. His writing won many more honors than I have space to list here. But the responses from other writers, many of them renowned, are so remarkable I must include a few.

The great Ian Frazier said that Brian "wrote more powerfully about faith than anyone in his generation." The peripatetic and contemplative Pico Iyer: "Almost nobody has written with the joy, the galloping energy, the quiet love of conscience and family and what's best in us, the living optimism." Renowned albatross savior Hob Osterlund: "He knew the strength of women without reduction, without fear or pretense, without the need to saint." The late Mary Oliver on his essays: "They were all favorites." (And for a Catholic writer to have his work chosen for *Best American Essays* by Mary Oliver *and* by the famous atheist Christopher Hitchens bespeaks BD's extreme range of appeal.) "We love him," writes philosopher and earth defender Kathleen Dean Moore: "Brian gets fan mail, sure, but also love letters....People love his work, but more than that, they truly love him. We love him because he spreads his arms and lets us into his amazing mind and boundless heart....The moments he shares with us sing of adoration for all the whistling, sobbing, surging creation...[and] by opening our hearts without breaking them he answers our deepest yearning for meaning. Which is joy. Which is gratitude."

How in heaven's name did one man win such strikingly intimate praise? I would suggest that the extreme intimacy of his nonfiction was not only delightful but highly contagious. BD saw his stories as "diving boards, not news reports." He was interested less in "ostensible fact and nominal accuracy" than in "the bends and layers and implications and insinuations and shimmers of memory." Within those shimmers, he said, were "the seeds of stories to which other people can connect."

A far less subtle feature of Brian's sentence-making: when he intuited the approaching roar of a whitewater rapid in his imagination, he paddled steady on, refusing to portage round even the wildest water. The prose that resulted made timid readers feel as though they'd been thrown into a kayak and sent careering down a literary equivalent of Idaho's Payette River during spring runoff. But sentences that alarm the timid by awakening them to the wilder possibilities of language are *heightened,* not inept. BD played fast and loose with sentence length, rhythms, grammar, alliteration, and diction to disburden a heart and mind burgeoning with empathy, quickness, joy, wit, and love of "the sinuous riverine lewd amused pop and song of the American language." Calling a foul on such phrases is like disallowing certain three-point shots of BD's Golden State Warrior hero, Steph Curry, because they were launched so ridiculously far from the basket. If the ball goes through the hoop and if the sentence sings, both of them count, and I'm giving BD himself the last word on this matter, his ten exclamation points included:

From: Doyle, Brian
Subject: a ha!!!!!!!!!!
Date: January 2, 2015 at 11:34:43 AM MST
To: David Duncan

Have you ever paid attention to Tolstoy's language? Enormous sentences, one clause piled on top of another. Do not think this is accidental, that it is a flaw. It is art, and it is achieved through hard work.

—Anton Chekhov

Brian Doyle lived the pleasure of bearing daily witness to quiet glories hidden in people, places, and creatures of little or no size, renown, or commercial value, and he brought inimitably playful or soaring or aching or heartfelt language to his tellings. When he finished a nonfiction gem he stacked it in his study until he had built up a modest but serviceable book manuscript, which he mailed off without fuss, usually to very small religious publishers. Many of BD's friends, myself included, felt that by scattering his best nonfiction through thirteen modest volumes over the years, he prevented his nonfiction from winning the national repute it deserved. This, coupled with his financial fears for his family after his tumor was diagnosed, is why, shortly after his first devastating brain surgery, I asked BD's permission to consolidate, in a single volume, the kind of nonfiction that earned the extreme praise I've quoted from friends, fans, and editors of magazines, with all proceeds to go to his family. Brian did not say yes. He said, "Sweet Jesus, YES!...Take whatever you want and tell whatever stories you want."

With that blessing in hand, I set about assembling this manuscript with two magnificent co-editors: the editor-in-chief of *Orion* magazine, H. Emerson (Chip) Blake, and the writer Kathleen (Katie) Yale. BD's nonfiction appeared more than any other writer's in *Orion,* and Chip and I had worked together on my *Orion* writing for years. Katie also worked for *Orion,* including on many of the BD pieces, and she knew his work more widely and deeply than Chip and I did, making her the perfect guide in our efforts. To commune with our friend on this project became a joy to all three of us.

Speaking of my own friendship with Brian: when we met twenty-five years ago we each experienced, without overtly acknowledging it, a flame in each of us that we could always find burning in the other; a flame we both held to be inextinguishable. We recognized our shared willingness to speak of almost anything we perceived as spiritual truth. We also loved, during our afternoon work doldrums, to share stuff and nonsense of no redeeming social or spiritual value whatsoever. In response, for instance, to a random baseball note from me about how terrifying it must have been for batters to face the six-foot-ten-inch pitcher Randy Johnson, whose wingspan was so wide and fastball so fast he seemed to reach out and set his pitches in the catcher's mitt by hand, BD instantly replied that Johnson towered atop a mound "like a stork on acid," whereas Roger Clemens, since our topic was terror, "*hulked* on the mound, like a supersized wolverine with hemorrhoids." I received 530 such emails and 200 snail-mail notes and missives from BD in our last two years alone, and sent back close to the same. We shot "riverine lewd amused pop and song" back and forth the way tournament table tennis players exchange shots: for the high-speed joy of it.

That joy was so important to us both that, a few weeks after BD's death, it felt perfectly natural to sit down and write him yet another letter. In this one I recalled an exchange, via our usual email Ping-Pong, in which we marveled that the bodies of trees are built by their downward hunger for earth and water *and* by their upward yearning for light. How wonderful, we agreed, that these paradoxical aims, instead of tearing a tree in two or causing it to die of indecision, cause it to grow tall and strong. And just as wonderful, I wrote to my flown friend, is how "during the tree's afterlife, its former hunger and yearning transmogrifies into the enduring structural integrity known as wood. Wood is a tree's life history become something so solid that we can hold it in our hands. This is not just some lonely cry or mournful eulogy. Right here in the world where every living thing dies, a fallen tree's integrity remains so literal that if a luthier adds strings to it, we can turn the departed tree's sun-yearning and thirst-quenching into the sounds we call live music. And if a seeming lunatic smashes wood's integrity to a pulp, then makes that pulp into paper, our ink can bring to life stories that multitudes can perform like symphonies in the sanctums of their very own depths and heights."

It's a great solace to me to imagine how many readers have done exactly that with Brian's stories, and how many more will have that experience in this book.

In a tribute in *Christian Century*, Jonathan Hiskes quotes Brian calling his writing "the attempt to stare God in the eye." As BD's spiritual intimate over his last six years, I feel this touches the very heart of his aim. Brian's work, Hiskes writes,

> was a mystical project born of both joy and desperation.... The whirling adjectives, aphorisms, metaphors and paradoxes were his method of using every tool he could to excavate the rich seams of the examined life. He wanted more than to stare God in the eye. He wanted to tell God a few things, and listen too. I

picture him as a songwriter-king dancing before his Lord, pouring out words, intermingling praise, grief, fury and laughter. The audacity makes me cringe. Then it draws me in.

Me too. Brian was a born cultural Catholic who cheerfully observed the rites of his inherited tradition. He also, sometimes audaciously, challenged his tradition, and he and I often whispered of our reverence for certain anything-but-orthodox humans and mystical texts. Three such for him were His Holiness the Dalai Lama, Thomas à Kempis's *The Imitation of Christ,* and the apocryphal *Gospel of Thomas,* in which Jesus's mysticism is so overt it's impossible for the Church to apply it to imperialistic ends. Three such for me are the excommunicated mystical genius Meister Eckhart, the thirteenth-century Zen master Eihei Dogen, and that same *Gospel of Thomas.*

During his final years, BD bravely bore intimations of an early departure from this life. During the same years he experienced ever-more-frequent visitations of what I can only call epiphanic joys. In the last lines of his last book, *Eight Whopping Lies and Other Stories of Bruised Grace,* BD summons his combined desperation and joy when he does not merely quote but *lives* à Kempis's recommended imitation, making Jesus's words in the Gospel of Thomas his own, praying to become, as a posthumous mystery, an unending prayer for his family. What greater gift can a mortal father possibly offer?

"We're only here for a minute," Brian once reminded us. "We're here for a little window. And to use that time to catch and share shards of light and laughter and grace seems to me the great story." How supreme he was at telling that story, and what a marvelous companion he was to so many. "I want to write to you like I'm speaking to you," he said. "I would sing my books if I could."

I say he could, and he did.

Watching Brian's heart songs pour out, relishing his whitewater sentences, too, I witnessed a daring writer and friend embodying the sublime paradox that Dogen described in these words: "The path of water is not noticed by water, it is realized by water.... To study the way is to study the self, to study the self is to forget the self, to forget the self is to awaken into the ten thousand things." As much as any man or woman I've ever known, Brian James Patrick Doyle reveled in the act of awakening into the ten thousand things.

—*DJD, Lolo, Montana, February 25, 2019*

I.

That the Small Is Huge,
That the Tiny Is Vast, That
Pain Is Part and Parcel of
the Gift of Joy, and That
This Is Love

Joyas Voladoras

Consider the hummingbird for a long moment. A hummingbird's heart beats ten times a second. A hummingbird's heart is the size of a pencil eraser. A hummingbird's heart is a lot of the hummingbird. *Joyas voladoras,* flying jewels, the first white explorers in the Americas called them, and the white men had never seen such creatures, for hummingbirds came into the world only in the Americas, nowhere else in the universe, more than three hundred species of them whirring and zooming and nectaring in hummer time zones nine times removed from ours, their hearts hammering faster than we could clearly hear if we pressed our elephantine ears to their infinitesimal chests.

Each one visits a thousand flowers a day. They can dive at sixty miles an hour. They can fly backward. They can fly more than five hundred miles without pausing to rest. But when they rest they come close to death: on frigid nights, or when they are starving, they retreat into torpor, their metabolic rate slowing to a fifteenth of their normal sleep rate, their hearts sludging nearly to a halt, barely beating, and if they are not soon warmed, if they do not soon find that which is sweet, their hearts grow cold, and they cease to be. Consider for a moment those hummingbirds who did not open their eyes again today, this very day, in the Americas: bearded helmetcrests and booted racket-tails, violet-tailed sylphs and violet-capped woodnymphs, crimson topazes and purple-crowned fairies, red-tailed comets and amethyst woodstars, rainbow-bearded thornbills and glittering-bellied emeralds, velvet-purple coronets and golden-bellied starfrontlets, fiery-tailed awlbills and Andean hillstars, spatuletails and pufflegs, each the most amazing thing you have never seen, each thunderous wild heart the size of an infant's fingernail, each mad heart silent, a brilliant music stilled.

Hummingbirds, like all flying birds but more so, have incredible enormous immense ferocious metabolisms. To drive those metabolisms they have race-car hearts that eat oxygen at an eye-popping rate. Their hearts are built of thinner, leaner fibers than ours. Their arteries are stiffer and more taut. They have more mitochondria in their heart muscles—anything to gulp more oxygen. Their hearts are stripped to the skin for the war against gravity and inertia, the mad search for food, the insane idea of flight. The price of their ambition is a life closer to death; they suffer more heart attacks and aneurysms and ruptures than any other living creature. It's expensive to fly. You burn out. You fry the machine. You melt the engine. Every creature on earth has approximately two billion heartbeats to spend in a lifetime. You can spend them slowly, like a tortoise, and live to be two hundred years old, or you can spend them fast, like a hummingbird, and live to be two years old.

The biggest heart in the world is inside the blue whale. It weighs more than seven tons. It's as big as a room. It *is* a small room, with four chambers. A child could walk around in it, head high, bending only to step through the valves. The valves are as big as the swinging doors in a saloon. This house of a heart drives a creature a hundred feet long. When this creature is born it is twenty feet long and weighs four tons. It is waaaaay bigger than your car. It drinks a hundred gallons of milk from its mama every day and gains two hundred pounds a day, and when it is seven or eight years old it endures an unimaginable puberty and then it essentially disappears from human ken, for next to nothing is known of the mating habits, travel patterns, diet, social life, language, social structure, diseases, spirituality, wars, stories, despairs, and arts of the blue whale. There are perhaps ten thousand blue whales in the world, living in every ocean on earth, and of the largest animal who ever lived we know nearly nothing. But we know this: the animals with the largest hearts in the world generally travel in pairs, and their penetrating moaning cries, their piercing yearning tongue, can be heard underwater for miles and miles.

Mammals and birds have hearts with four chambers. Reptiles and turtles have hearts with three chambers. Fish have hearts with two chambers. Insects and mollusks have hearts with one chamber. Worms have hearts with one chamber, although they may have as many as eleven single-chambered hearts. Unicellular bacteria have no hearts at all; but even they have fluid eternally in motion, washing from one side of the cell to the other, swirling and whirling. No living being is without interior liquid motion. We all churn inside.

So much held in a heart in a lifetime. So much held in a heart in a day, an hour, a moment. We are utterly open with no one in the end— not mother and father, not wife or husband, not lover, not child, not friend. We open windows to each but we live alone in the house of the heart. Perhaps we must. Perhaps we could not bear to be so naked, for fear of a constantly harrowed heart. When young we think there will come one person who will savor and sustain us always; when we are older we know this is the dream of a child, that all hearts finally are bruised and scarred, scored and torn, repaired by time and will, patched by force of character, yet fragile and rickety forevermore, no matter how ferocious the defense and how many bricks you bring to the wall. You can brick up your heart as stout and tight and hard and cold and impregnable as you possibly can and down it comes in an instant, felled by a woman's second glance, a child's apple breath, the shatter of glass in the road, the words *I have something to tell you,* a cat with a broken spine dragging itself into the forest to die, the brush of your mother's papery ancient hand in the thicket of your hair, the memory of your father's voice early in the morning echoing from the kitchen where he is making pancakes for his children.

A Shrew

One time a long time ago when I was supple and strong and rubbery
As a snake in a hurry I was on my belly in the bush and saw a shrew
In the litter of leaves and for the longest shortest moment we startled
Each other considerably but maybe the scale of our encounter was so
Ludicrously unbalanced that our normal fear of weird missed the bus,
Leaving us eye to eye under the epic ambition of a huckleberry tangle.
I remember thinking that the shrew was awfully near my two absolute
Favorite eyeballs and that shrews are said to be terrors among the tiny.
I remember that it was the size of a thumb or a thimble or a little cigar.
I remember that it had a lustrous dense shining coat as black as can be.
I remember wondering even then what it could possibly be wondering.
I remember that he or she seemed to be missing a northeast appendage.
Many questions and angles of inquiry presented themselves to me later,
Such as what combination of factors could deduct a limb from a shrew,
And what manner of beast could have executed said deletion—perhaps
A romantic tangle, a political wrangle, a religious debate turned savage
As so often has been the case? Or the usual suspects snuffling for meat.
Or maybe shrews, who do not live long in the way the world calculates,
Dissolve a leg at a time, growing ever closer to the sensuous roil of soil,
As do we all. But meanwhile there's such a hungry immediacy, correct?
All these years later that's what I remember from that shrewish moment,
That I stopped thinking and just stared. Yes, partly because I was scared,
But there was something beyond curiosity or the startle of astonishment.
For just an instant I paid attention with every shard and iota of my being.

Maybe we couldn't survive if we were like that all the time, I don't know, But when it happens we see that which none of us can find the words for. Sometimes we are starving to see every bit of what is right in front of us.

Tigers

I am standing in the hospital watching babies emerge from my wife like a circus act. First one out is a boy, dark-haired and calm, the size of an owl. He is immediately commandeered by a nurse who whisks him off for a bath and a stint in what appears to be a tiny tanning bed. Now, says the doctor, reaching around inside my wife while he talks, here's the other one, and he hauls out another boy. This one is light-haired and not calm; he grabs for a nurse's scissors and won't let go and they have to pry his fingers off and the nurse looks accusingly at me for some reason and I want to say hey, I don't even know the guy, but I don't say anything, being overwhelmed with new roommates and tears and astonishment at people emerging from my wife one after another like a circus act.

This boy, the second one, the burglar, turns out to have a major problem. He's missing a chamber in his heart. You need four chambers and most people get four, but he gets only three and there's no one to whom I can complain so they have to fix him, otherwise he dies.

Fixing him entails cutting open his chest with a saw and prying the chest bone open with a tool that looks like the Jaws of Life and chilling his heart with a bucket of ice and hooking him up to a machine that continues to pump his blood and some of mine through his brain and body while the surgeon reroutes his veins.

I ask if I can hold him in my lap during the operation, just to have my skin on his skin while he goes off to another planet while they fix him, but they say no.

Outside the hospital window I see three crows dogging a hawk.

The hawk flinches when they flare by his head, he ducks and rolls and hunches his shoulders, but he doesn't leave the tree. His troubles are inches from his face but he glares and waits, stolid, angry, churning, his thoughts sharp as razors, his brain filled with blood and meat.

The operation was really two operations, it turns out, and the doctors did the first one pretty soon after he was born, and that operation went by in a blur. Then comes a second operation when he is almost two years old, and that goes by in a blur, too, though I remember a nurse praying by his crib at four in the morning when I got up to pray by his crib.

A day after his second operation the doctors tell me I can try to feed him real food, the food he likes, which is peas.

So here I am feeding him in his hospital bed. The bed is cantilevered up at the north end so that he can eat. He is eating pea by pea. He is awake but groggy and each time a pea hovers into his viewfinder he regards it with sluggish surprise. He likes peas. I put the peas in his mouth one by one. His lips reach out a little for each pea and then maul it gently for a while before the pea disappears. Each time his lips accept the pea they also accept the ends of my thumb and forefinger for an instant. After thirteen peas he falls asleep and I crank the bed back flat and kneel down and pray like hell.

Next day the doctors say I can heft him gently out of his bed and hold him, just be careful with all the wires and tubes. There are a lot of wires and tubes. There is a heart monitor running from his chest to a machine the size of a dryer. There is a breathing tube planted in his nose. There is a blood pressure monitor attached to his big toe. There is a drainage tube running from his chest to a clear plastic box on the end of his bed. The box fills twice a day with blood and water. There is a tube in his neck, in his carotid artery. This tube runs nowhere. It's for emergencies. It's the tube through which the doctors would cram major drugs in case the surgical repair of his heart fails, slumps over, gives out, blows a tire, gives up the ghost, kicks the bucket, hits the wall, buys the farm.

I lift him out of the bed. He whimpers and moans. I feel like my

9

fingers are knives on him, but I fold him into my lap and we settle back into the recliner and arrange the wires and tubes so that no machines are beeping. I grab the clicker and flip on the television, which hangs from the ceiling like a goiter. Click bass fishing click talk show click infomercial click news click nature show click basketball game click sitcom click commercial at which point the boy who has been slumped in my lap like a dozing seal suddenly reaches for the clicker, startling me; I thought he was asleep. But no—he punches away at the clicker with his thumb and back down the channels we go, click sitcom click basketball game click nature show, which is about tigers, and having arrived at the tigers he wanted to see, he stops clicking, leans back in my lap again, and laughs!, a guttural chortle, a deep-in-the-throat guffaw, a basso huh huh huh, and a great sob rises in me suddenly, and for the next few minutes as we watch the massive grace and power and patience of tigers I cry like the baby he used to be before all these tubes and wires, because this is the first time he's laughed in weeks, and he is going to be fine, and everything is suddenly over.

A few minutes later he grows tired of tigers and the excitement of being out of bed and I put him back in the bed and arrange his nest of wires and tubes, and he is already asleep by the time I flip out the light and stand against the window and lean forward and touch the window with my face and think about hawks and tigers, and pray like crazy.

Leap

A couple leaped from the South Tower, hand in hand. They reached for each other and their hands met and they jumped.

Jennifer Brickhouse saw them falling, hand in hand.

Many people jumped. Perhaps hundreds. No one knows. They struck the pavement with such force that there was a pink mist in the air.

The mayor reported the mist.

A kindergarten boy who saw people falling in flames told his teacher that the birds were on fire. She ran with him on her shoulders out of the ashes.

Tiffany Keeling saw fireballs falling that she later realized were people. Jennifer Griffin saw people falling and wept as she told the story. Niko Winstral saw people free-falling backward with their hands out, like they were parachuting. Joe Duncan on his roof on Duane Street looked up and saw people jumping. Henry Weintraub saw people "leaping as they flew out." John Carson saw six people fall, "falling over themselves, falling, they were somersaulting." Steve Miller saw people jumping from a thousand feet in the air. Kirk Kjeldsen saw people flailing on the way down, people lining up and jumping, "too many people falling." Jane Tedder saw people leaping and the sight haunts her at night. Steve Tamas counted fourteen people jumping and then he stopped counting. Stuart De-Hann saw one woman's dress billowing as she fell, and he saw a shirtless man falling end over end, and he too saw the couple leaping hand in hand.

Several pedestrians were killed by people falling from the sky. A fireman was killed by a body falling from the sky.

But he reached for her hand and she reached for his hand and they leaped out the window holding hands.

I try to whisper prayers for the sudden dead and the harrowed families of the dead and the screaming souls of the murderers but I keep coming back to his hand and her hand nestled in each other with such extraordinary ordinary succinct ancient naked stunning perfect simple ferocious love.

Their hands reaching and joining are the most powerful prayer I can imagine, the most eloquent, the most graceful. It is everything that we are capable of against horror and loss and death. It is what makes me believe that we are not craven fools and charlatans to believe in God, to believe that human beings have greatness and holiness within them like seeds that open only under great fires, to believe that some unimaginable essence of who we are persists past the dissolution of what we were, to believe against such evil hourly evidence that love is why we are here.

No one knows who they were: husband and wife, lovers, dear friends, colleagues, strangers thrown together at the window there at the lip of hell. Maybe they didn't even reach for each other consciously, maybe it was instinctive, a reflex, as they both decided at the same time to take two running steps and jump out the shattered window, but they did reach for each other, and they held on tight, and leaped, and fell endlessly into the smoking canyon, at two hundred miles an hour, falling so far and so fast that they would have blacked out before they hit the pavement near Liberty Street so hard that there was a pink mist in the air.

Jennifer Brickhouse saw them holding hands, and Stuart DeHann saw them holding hands, and I hold on to that.

Two Hearts

Some months ago my wife delivered twin sons one minute apart. The older is Joseph and the younger is Liam. Joseph is dark and Liam is light. Joseph is healthy and Liam is not. Joseph has a whole heart and Liam has half. This means that Liam will have two major surgeries before he is three years old. The first surgery—during which a doctor will slice open my son's chest with a razor, saw his breastbone in half, and reconstruct the flawed plumbing of his heart—is imminent.

I have read many pamphlets about Liam's problem. I have watched many doctors' hands drawing red and blue lines on pieces of white paper. They are trying to show me why Liam's heart doesn't work properly. Blue lines are for blood that needs oxygen. Red lines are for blood that needs to be pumped out of the heart. I watch the markers in the doctors' hands. Here comes red, there goes blue. The heart is a railroad station where the trains are switched to different tracks. A normal heart switches trains flawlessly two billion times in a life; in an abnormal heart, like Liam's, the trains crash and the station crumbles to dust.

There are many nights just now when I tuck Liam and his wheezing train station under my beard in the blue hours of night and think about his Maker. I would kill the god who sentenced him to such awful pain, I would stab him in the heart like he stabbed my son, I would shove my fury in his face like a fist, but I know in my own broken heart that this same god made my magic boys, shaped their apple faces and coyote eyes, put joy in the eager suck of their mouths.

So it is that my hands are not clenched in anger but clasped in confused and merry and bitter prayer.

I talk to God more than I admit. "Why did you break my boy?" I ask.

I gave you that boy, He says, and his lean brown brother, and the elfin daughter you love so.

"But you wrote death on his heart," I say.

I write death on all hearts, He says, just as I write life.

This is where our conversation always ends, and I am left holding the extraordinary awful perfect prayer of my second son, who snores like a seal, who might die tomorrow, who did not die today.

The Deceased

Imeasure the body with a ruler. The deceased is eight inches long and five inches wide if we count arm-span. There's not much in the way of arm-span. Mostly the arms are hands. The hands look eerily like baseball gloves. The teeth are tiny but populous and adamant. The tail is stubbish and not a tail you would boast about if you were in a pub and the talk turned to boasting about tails. It's more of a fleshy rudder than a tail. The eyes are small and black and open. I look in vain for ears. The nose is epic and tremendous and clearly what the face was designed to carry much like a ship carries a prow. I refrain from trying to ascertain gender, out of respect for the dignity of the deceased.

The deceased is, I believe, *Scapanus townsendii,* the Townsend's mole, native to this region, found everywhere from swampland to small mountains; but as soon as I read the parade of Latin labels by which it is classified, and wade through discussions of its economic impact on farm and pasture and garden, and its former commercial value (coats and muffs and waistcoats made of mole fur were once popular, partly because mole fur has no "grain," as do other animal pelts), I begin to ponder the minimal substance of our labels and commentary on this and all other of our neighbors, and I wonder about this particular individual, and the flavor and tenor and yearning of this one life, and long I stand over its sprawled body, leaning on the shovel by which it will soon be returned unto the earth that was its home and heart.

With sincere respect for Mr. John Townsend of Philadelphia, who wandered thoroughly in the forests and mountains of the West, paying such close attention to the beings therein that he is credited with "discovering" plovers and swifts and warblers and thrashers and squirrels and bats and voles and chipmunks and this one tribe of mole, and who died young, merely forty-one, having slowly and unwittingly poisoned himself with the arsenic he used in preserving the animals he killed so as to study them more closely, I wonder what this particular mole at my feet called itself, or was called; how was it addressed, or thought of, or perceived, by its fellows? Was it a father, a grandfather, a great-great-grandfather? It is thought that this tribe of mole generally resides in home territories the size of a baseball field, and defends home court with remarkable ferocity, and that its children are generally born as spring begins, and that the children mature rapidly, and leave home as soon as they can, so that the family cavern, which is lined with a deep soft dense blanket of grass, and is accessible by as many as eleven tunnels running in every direction, is empty by the end of spring, and I stand here with the shovel thinking of the parents, proud of their progeny, but now bereft of their spirited company, and now alone in their echoing nest, busying themselves with quotidian duty; and soon this will be me, trying not to call our children every day, trying to celebrate their independence, trying not to wallow in memory.

This tribe of mole is thought to be largely solitary, I read, and I want to laugh and weep, as we are all largely solitary, and spend whole lifetimes digging tunnels toward each other, do we not? And sometimes we connect, thrilled and confused, sure and unsure at once, for a time, before the family cavern empties, or one among us does not come home at all, and faintly far away we hear the sound of the shovel.

I should toss the body over the fence, into the thicket, as food for the many, such being the language of life, but I think of how we feel when we are tucked tight in bed, inside the cocoon of the blankets, wrapped and rapt, and I wonder if moles love the grip of earth that way, love the press and dense of it, its inarguable weight, the blind swim through the dark, would love finally to dissolve in it; and I bury the body.

Eating Dirt

I have a small daughter and two smaller sons, twins. They are all three in our minuscule garden at the moment, my sons eating dirt as fast as they can get it off the planet and down their gullets. They are two years old, they were seized with dirt-fever an instant ago, and as admirably direct and forceful young men, quick to act, true sons of the West, they are going to eat some dirt, boy, and you'd better step aside.

My daughter and I step aside.

The boys are eating so much dirt so fast that much of it is missing their maws and sliding muddily down their chicken chests.... I watch a handful as it travels. It's rich brown stuff, almost black, crumbly. In a moment I will pull the boy over and issue a ticket, but right now I watch with interest as he inserts the dirt, chews meditatively, emits a wriggling worm, stares at it—and eats it, too.

"Dad, they're eating the garden!" says my daughter.

So they are and I'll stop them, soon. But for this rare minute in life... I feel, inarticulately, that there's something simple and true going on. Because we all eat dirt. Fruits and vegetables are dirt transformed by light and water. Animals are vigorous dirt, having dined on fruit, vegetables, or other animals who are dirt. Our houses, schools, offices are cupped by dirt and made of wood, stone, and brick—former dirt. Glass is largely melted sand, a kind of clean dirt. Our clothing used to be dirt. Paper was trees was dirt.... We breathe dirt suspended in the air, crunch it between our teeth on spinach leaves... wear it in the lines of our hands and folds of our faces, catch it in... our noses, eyes, ears. We swim in an ocean of regular normal orthodox there-it-sits-under-everything dirt.

18

The children tire, sun retreats, in we go to wash the garden off my sons. It swirls down the bath drain, into the river, eventually to the ocean…ends up as silt…sinks to the ocean floor…becomes kelp, razor clams, sea otters…rises, is drawn up into rain, and returns to our garden after its unimaginable vacation.

My daughter and I discuss these journeys. And when the rain begins we draw a map—which we leave on the back porch—so our dirt will know how to come home to our house.

"Maybe there are dirt fairies," says my daughter. "Or maybe dirt can read."

Maybe my daughter is right. Consider this essay, made by dirt worked in wondrous ways into bone, blood, protein, water, synaptic electricity, and words. So why couldn't dirt read and write? Why couldn't dirt lean against a fence with smaller lovelier dirt in his lap, and watch twin dirt demons devour dirt while the world spins in its miraculous mysterious circles, ashes to ashes, dust to dust, without end?

The Anchoviad

My daughter, age 6, sleeps with her bear, also age 6. My son, age 3, sleeps with his basketball and a stuffed tiger, age unknown. My other son, also age 3, sleeps with a can of anchovy fillets—King Oscar brand, caught off Morocco and distributed by the H. J. Nosaki Company in New York.

He sleeps with the can every night, won't go to sleep without it under his right cheek. The can is bright red and features a drawing of King Oscar, an avuncular, bearded fellow, apparently a benevolent despot. Every night, after Liam is asleep, I gently delete the can from his grip and examine it. It's a roll-key can, 56 grams, with "about six fillets (15 g)." Other than the friendly visage of King Oscar, my favorite thing about the can is the word *about,* a rare corporate concession to ambiguity. I suppose it's a legal thing, but still it pleases me, for murky reasons.

I sit there in the dark, holding the anchovies, and ponder other murky things, like: What's the deal with this boy and his anchovies? How is it that we are drawn to the odd things we love? How did anchovies from Morocco come to be swimming headless under my son's cheek in Oregon? What do we know about anchovies other than their savory saltiness? What do we really know well about any creature, including most of all ourselves, and how is it that even though we know painfully little about anything, we often manage world-wrenching hubris about our wisdom?

Consider the six animals in the can. Anchovies are members of the family Engraulidae, which range in size from a Brazilian anchovy the

20

size of your thumbnail to a ravenous New Guinea anchovy as long as your forearm. Anchovies don't survive in captivity, and they don't survive long after being netted, either, so we know little about them—but the little we know is riveting:

— Their hearing is perhaps the sharpest of any marine animal's, and the frequency they hear best is eerily, exactly the frequency of the tailbeats of other fish. Is it with the aid of their unimaginably crisp hearing that they manage to swim in darting collectives that twist as one astonishing creature? We don't know.

— Their noses contain a sensory organ that no other creature in the world has. What's it for? No one knows.

— Sensory complexes in anchovies' heads also form dense nets in the cheeks. What do these nets do? A puzzle.

— Anchovies get their food by dragging their open mouths through the ocean in mammoth schools, but what, exactly, do they eat? Surprise: No one knows.

Among the species of anchovy are, to the delight of meditative fathers sitting on their sons' beds in the dark, the buccaneer anchovy (which travels farthest into the open ocean) and the sabretooth anchovy, which has very large teeth and hangs around, understandably, by itself. And I do not even mention the anchovies' cousin, the wolf herring, which grows to be a yard long and has so many teeth that it has teeth on its tongue.

Thus the anchovy is fully as mysterious a creature as, well, as this boy sleeping with the fishes. And what, really, do I know irrefutably about my son? Some of his quirks, a bit of his character, his peculiar dietary habits, the lilt of his song, the ache of his sob, where his scars are, the way his hair wants to go, the knock of his knees—and not much else. He is a startling, one-time-only, boneheaded miracle with a sensory complex in his head and heart that I can only guess at and dimly try to savor in the few brilliant moments I have been given to swim with him. He is a sort of anchovy, as are we all; so I sing our collective salty song—the song of fast, mysterious, open-mouthed creatures, traveling with vast schools of our fellows, listening intently, savoring the least of our brethren, and doing our absolute level best to avoid the wolf herring.

Illuminos

One child held on to my left pinky finger everywhere we went. Never any other finger and never the right pinky but only the left pinky and never my whole hand. My finger misses her hand this morning. It has been many years since she held my finger. To this day sometimes in the morning when I dress I stare at my left pinky and suddenly I am in the playground, or on the beach, or in a thrumming crowd, and there is a person weighing forty pounds holding on to my left pinky so tightly that I am tacking slightly to port. I miss tacking slightly to port.

Another child held on to my left trouser leg most of the time but he would, if he deemed it necessary, hold either of my hands, and one time both of my hands, when we were shuffling in the surf, and the water was up to my knees but up to his waist, and I walked along towing him like a small grinning chortling dinghy all the way from the sea cave where we thought there might be sea lions sleeping off a salmon bender to the tide pools where you could find starfish and crabs and anemones and mussels the size of your shoes.

The third child held hands happily all the time, either hand, any hand, my hands, his mother's hands, his brother's hands, his sister's hands, his friends, aunts and uncles and cousins and grandparents and teachers, dogs and trees, neighbors and bushes, he would hold hands with any living creature whatsoever, without the slightest trepidation or self-consciousness, and to this day I admire that boy's open genuine eager unadorned verve. He once held hands with his best friend during

22

an entire soccer game when they were five years old, the two of them running in tandem, or one starting in one direction unbeknownst to the other and down they both went giggling in the sprawl of the grass. It seems to me that angels and bodhisattvas are everywhere available for consultation if only we can see them clear; they are unadorned, and joyous, and patient, and radiant, and luminous, and not disguised or hidden or filtered in any way whatsoever, so that if you see them clearly, which happens occasionally even to the most blinkered and frightened of us, you realize immediately who they are, beings of great and humble illumination dressed in the skins of new and dewy beings, and you realize, with a catch in your throat, that they are your teachers, and they are agents of an unimaginable love, and they are your cousins and companions in awe, and they are miracles and prayers and songs of inexplicable beauty whom no one can explain and no one own or claim or trammel, and that simply to perceive them is to be blessed beyond the reach of language, and that to be the one appointed to tow them along a beach, or a crowd, or home through the brilliant morning from the muddy hilarious peewee soccer game is to be graced beyond measure or understanding; which is what I was, and I am, and I will be, until the day I die, and change form from this one to another, in ways miraculous and mysterious, never to be plumbed by the mind or measures of man.

II.

There Was a Kid Who Was and Isn't But Is

Times Tables

Just got a note from my mom in which she tells me
That my gentle wry witty subtle sister, now resident
In a monastery, used to rock my cradle with her foot
While chanting her multiplication tables aloud. How
I would love to report that I remember every blessed
Moment of this, how my sister tried to achieve a sort
Of whispered chant (loud enough to be articulate but
Soft enough not to wake me), how my mother would
Forget about us and get absorbed by heated table talk
About religions and wars and then realize with a start
That my sister was on her seventeenth run-through of
Her times tables, how my dad would smile and say O
Let her rip for another hour and the both of them will
Be math geniuses. But I don't remember. Or do I? Now
That I think about it, I worship rhythm and measure it
Unconsciously, automatically—I have an extra ear for
The cadence of crows, the coughing of motors, an owl
Calling sixteen times to another, who calls back seven:
And seven times sixteen equals a way to spell out love.

My Devils

One time when I was seven years old, my aunt placed her hands upon me and tried to drive out my devils. I was not aware that I had any resident devils and said so, hesitantly, as she was a firm woman. She said, *You certainly do have devils, and they are beginning to manifest.* I did not know what *manifest* meant but did not say so. She moved her hands from my head to my shoulders to my chest and then back up to my head again. I wanted to ask where the devils lived and how many there were and what they looked like and did they know Lucifer personally and was he a decent guy who just snapped one day or what, but she was intent and her eyes were closed and she was not a woman to be interrupted while she was working.

After a while she opened her eyes, and I asked if the devils were gone, and she said, *We will see, we will see.* Even then I knew that if someone said something twice it meant that they were not sure it was so. I was learning that a lot of times what people meant was not at all what they said. *Maybe* meant no, and *The Lord will provide* meant the Lord had not yet provided, and *Take your time* meant hurry up. It was hard to learn all the languages spoken in our house. There was the loose limber American language that we all spoke, and then there was the riverine sinuous Irish language that the old people spoke when they were angry, and then there was the chittery sparrowish female language that my mother and grandmother and aunts and the neighborhood women spoke, and then there was the raffish chaffing language that other dads spoke to my dad when they came over for cocktail parties, and then there was the high slow language we all spoke when priests were in the house, and then there were the dialects spoken by only one person—for example, my sister, who spoke the haughty languorous language of her many cats, or my youngest brother, Tommy, who spoke Tommy, which only he and my sister could understand. She would often translate for him; apparently he talked mostly about cheese and crayons.

The rest of that day I went around feeling filled with devils and slightly queasy about it. I figured they must be living in my stomach or lungs, because those were the only places inside me with any air to breathe. I asked my oldest brother if devils needed air, the way people do, and he made a gesture with his hand that meant *Go away right now*. Hand gestures were another language in our family, and our mother was the most eloquent speaker of that tongue. If she turned her hand one way it meant *Go get my cigarettes*. If she turned it another way it meant *What you just said is so silly that I am not going to bother to disabuse you of your idiocy*. Still other gestures meant *Whatever*, and *In a thousand years it will all be the same*, and *Take your youngest brother with you and do not attempt to give me lip about it*.

I waited until bedtime to ask my mother about my devils. She was about to make the hand gesture that meant *We will talk about this some other time*, but then she saw my worried expression, and she stopped and sat down with me, and I explained about my aunt and the laying on of hands. My mother made a few incomprehensible sounds in her throat and then talked about her sister as if she were a tree that we were examining from various angles. Her sweet sister was a wonderfully devout person, she said, and she had the very best of intentions, and she had the truest heart of anyone you could ever meet, and she was more alert to the prevalence of miracles than anyone else my mother knew, and you had to admire the depth of her faith—we should all be as committed and dedicated and passionate as she was—but the fact was that we were not quite as committed as my aunt to the more remote possibilities, such as the laying on of hands to dispel demons. *Do you have the slightest idea what I am saying to you?* she asked. I said I did not, hesitantly, because I didn't want her to stop talking so beautifully and entertainingly, and she put her hand on my forehead and said that she loved me, and that it was bedtime, so I'd better hop to it, which I did. As she left, she made a gesture with her hand that meant *If you don't brush your teeth and then try to pretend that you did, I will know you are telling a lie and it will not end well,* and she laughed, and I laughed, and I brushed my teeth.

We Did

Did we punch and hammer and jab each other as children, thrashing and rambling, a large family in a small house filled with brothers and one older sister with bony fists and no reluctance to use them?

We did.

Did we use implements like long whippy maple branches and Mom's bamboo garden poles and Dad's old sagging tennis rackets and redolent pieces of oozy lumber stolen from the new house going up down the block and brick chips and sharp-edged asbestos shingles torn off the garage roof as ammunition and weaponry with which to battle and joust with brothers and occasionally the Murphy boys next door, each one burlier and angrier and Irisher than the next?

We did.

Did we occasionally use snowballs, meticulously packed as tight as possible and then placed carefully in the freezer for days, as stony ammunition despite the cold hard fact that said snowballs should have been registered with the United Nations, especially when one of us saved a few until June and hammered the Murphy boys in the most lopsided and glorious victory of all time on our street?

We did.

Did our mother actually say more than once, *You'll put your eye out!* until finally we bought individual glass eyes at a yard sale from an ophthalmologist and faked a terrific raucous brawl so that our mother came running only to find her sons roaring about their lost eyes, which were bouncing and rolling freely on the linoleum floor, which caused our blessed mother to shriek, which caused our calm muscular father to come running, which caused his sons to spend many hours in penitential labor and the mastermind to go to confession?

We did.

Did we play football so hard in the yard that more than once a helmet went flying and more than once a finger was broken and one time tempers flared such that a picket from the old red fence was used for assault and battery?

We did.

Did we play basketball so intently and furiously that a nose was broken and eyeglasses were broken and teeth were chipped and skin was abraded and fouls were delivered with violent intent, which was repaid in full in the fullness of time?

We did.

Did we many times wrestle our oldest and tallest brother to the ground, often using our youngest brother as a missile aimed at his feet to knock him off balance, and once the tree was toppled, jump upon him with cheerful violent alacrity, and pile on with as much emphasis as humanly possible, sometimes leaping off the couch to cannonball down upon him, while ignoring the plaintive murmur of our youngest brother trapped at the bottom of the pile, mewling like a kitten?

We did.

Did we occasionally reach or lunge across the table during meals to commit crimes upon the bodies of our brothers, even though Dad had said, and he meant it, too, that the next boy who reached across the table would lose a finger?

We did.

We did all these things and more, and you would think the accumulated violence would have bred dislike or bitterness or vengeful urges, but I report with amazement that it did not. Yes, the trundle of years and the fading of memory are at play. Yes, we are all much older and slower and have lost the language of pummel and lash. Yes, we have all witnessed and endured pain and loss in such doses that the wounds of our brotherly years seem minor now compared to the larger darkness.

But there is something else here. Maybe, in some strange way I don't understand, we used our hands to say the things we didn't have the words to say. That is what I have tried to do with my hands and my words this morning, brothers. Remember the crash of bodies, and the grapple in the grass, and the laughing pile on the rug, for that was the thrum of our love.

So let us now arise, and haul our youngest brother out from the bottom of the pile by his thin flailing legs, and restore him to a semblance of his usual shape, and proceed to the dinner table, chaffing and shouldering, and it will always be this moment somehow, brothers, just before we eat, just before the tide of time rises, in the instant of silence just before Dad says grace.

The Sea

We were perhaps eight and ten, my brother and I, both invited to a house by the ocean, and that first night, after lots of hullabaloo, we were ladled into old summer camp cots that hadn't been used since Lincoln's time, and I remember, as if it was just last week, that we both felt something grim in the sea for the first time—a cold careless mastery, maybe. I still can't articulate this very well. We lay there listening to the infinitesimally tiny increase in wavelet volume as the tide came in, rustling acres of mussel shells and old boats and horseshoe crabs and the pots that jailed uncountable families of lobsters, and the *scents* sliding through the windows were loud, dense, lurid, something to smell gingerly and back away from. I was scared more than I would ever admit to my brother. We had been to the beach two million times, sure, but those were brilliant days, an ocean to taunt, not one that smelled like all deaths that ever were, marinated for a billion years and then sent smiling into canals and inlets. Low tide, people say, my god, what a stench, but to me it was more entrancing than I will ever be able to explain; it was sex and death and time, and every far corner of the planet, the liquors of all the lives that are and were, something ancient beyond any explanations, something that had always been there before even the uncountable lives that filled it now, something bigger than land, the biggest idea there is that you can touch or be drowned in, the biggest thing that's real, that's right here, that we can't dismiss or explain, or lie about. I never did forget that night. I was frightened and fascinated in about the same proportions. In a lot of ways we never did leave the ocean as a species, as shy naked mammals. It still sloshes around in our innermost rooms. You know exactly what I'm saying. You have stood there too, staring at it for reasons you can't explain. I believe that love is our greatest and hardest work.

Catch

One time when I was young, a thousand years ago, I decided to play baseball for the Catholic league team, even though I was terrified of the tiny rocky ball and did not at all understand the supposedly pastoral allure of the sport, which seemed painfully slow and jerky to me, and rather selfish to boot; as far as I could tell the pitcher surrendered the ball only with the greatest reluctance, after pondering the matter grimly for a long time and shaking his head testily at the catcher; and then when he did finally take leave of the ball he did so with unseemly petulance, flinging it angrily at the batter or the catcher or the umpire, hitting one or another of these poor unfortunates at every turn. Meanwhile the fielders fiddled with their private parts, or shouted fervid nonsensical things, or spat copiously into the dust, or pounded their mitts angrily, as if their poor cowhide gloves had done anything but idly gape as the pitcher seethed on the mound and fielders scratched their private parts and the umpire made inarticulate hooting sounds when the ball hit the backstop or batter or catcher or even the umpire hiding behind the catcher to provide a smaller target for the furious pitcher. All in all the game seemed peculiar to me, but several of my friends had decided to play, so I decided to play too.

Because I had never played before, my father pointed out to me that being generally unsure of baseball's regulations and what he called the rhythm and geometry of the game was a substantive drawback, and he offered to have a catch, so that I could understand the basic transaction of the sport, as he said, which is the exchange of the ball; everyone talks about *hitting*, he said, but hitters do not actually hit much or effectively, and even when they do manage to interrupt the ball before it hits the backstop or umpire, often it goes awry, which is called a fouled or vulgar ball, or it is hit directly at the fielders, who are expected to promptly defend themselves; so that learning to snare and share the ball is crucial, just as in your beloved basketball, although in baseball the actual ball is tiny and granitic, because the game is descended from cricket, which also has a tiny hard ball, probably because the English are a parsimonious and masochistic race, and actually enjoy affliction, which is a sin, and one reason their savage empire collapsed.

This was and is how my dad talks, which has provided endless education over the years; it was a great shock for us to discover, in late childhood, that other dads did not talk with this bemused sidelong imaginative twist, so that you would be entertained and epiphanated, as my sister once said, all at once, on any subject from empires to umpires and back again.

So out we went into the street for a catch, a remarkable fact for a number of reasons: my dad and I had never had a catch, neither of us had ever held or thrown a baseball, neither of us had ever worn cattle-skin hand guards, and the prospect was so amazing that all my brothers came out to see this also, and this flood of brothers was savory bait for the rest of the kids on the block, so that very soon there were dozens of children in the street gaping at *Mister Doyle!* with a *baseball glove!* on one hand and a *baseball!* in the other.

I should pause to explain again how unthinkable this was at that time on that street. The other dads in our neighborhood would occasionally lumber off their porches and trot heavily into the street and toss baseballs and footballs, wearing ragged sweatshirts and Old Man Pants and second-best shoes, but our dad had never set foot in the street between the tight rows of cars, and the very idea of him jumping off the porch and trotting into the street was beyond human imagination. *Our* dad was a tall dignified man of fifty who wore a fedora and an excellent topcoat when he strode briskly to the train along the sidewalk every morning on his way into the city to work as a journalist. He was erudite and witty and literary. He had read everything and wrote for magazines and was avuncular and wise and the kind of dad you turned to for quiet advice, the kind of dad whose most terrifying remark to his children was *Could I have a word with you?* He was not at all the kind of dad who leapt off the porch and trotted out into the street wearing a ragged sweatshirt, which is not to say that our dad was unathletic, or unfamiliar with brawn and sport and violence; he had been a college tennis player, then a sergeant and then lieutenant in the United States Army in not one but two wars, and he had at least once used his fists in anger, and he was well over six feet tall, and in the rare moments he was furious he had a grim glare that could peel paint. But those moments were so rare that they had become faint legends of long ago, now imperfectly remembered.

Then one spring afternoon he did step into the street, wearing a baseball glove he had found somewhere, and he did rear back and throw a baseball to me, and forty years later I can still see him as clear as if it was yesterday, standing tall and relaxed in the street, his shirt sleeves rolled up, his burly arm cocked to throw me the ball, dozens of children crowding as close as they could get to the street without actually being in it, to see no kidding *Mister Doyle!* throwing a baseball to *Brian*.

I cannot remember the number of successful exchanges of the tiny and granitic ball, signed by Ed Kranepool of the New York Mets; I believe it passed between us three or four times; let us say three, the number of aspects of God in the ancient religious tradition of our family. But on the fourth attempt, me being a boy with dense spectacles, awed by the weight of an unthinkable moment and murmuring crowd, I lost track of the ball as it left my father's hand. The ball hit me at what I remember as terrific velocity, in the right eye, and down I went, gibbering.

When my brothers and I tell this story now we concentrate on my subsequent incredible black eye (something of a misnomer, for blue and green and yellow were also involved), and on the miraculous fact that shards of glass did not pierce my eye and turn me into a larval cyclopean essayist, and on the way our dad went from a standing start thirty feet away to my side in an eighth of a second, and on how that early mishap proved all too predictive of my misadventures in baseball, in which I ended up a pitcher who hit the backstop or the batter or the umpire more than the catcher. But I have always preferred to celebrate the moment before the mishap, not the mishap itself. Mishaps are normal, but moments accompanied by children pouring out of their houses and crowding together along the curb to witness something they had never seen and would never see again are quiet miracles. A moment like that ought to be resurrected regularly, sung for the gift it is. When I do so, I have discovered, time dissolves, the past is present, and my dad is fifty again, and tall and bemused in the middle of the street between the tight rows of cars, and he rears back to whip the ball to me, and it's always hanging there, fresh from his hand, stunning.

The Meteorites

The summer I was eighteen, hardly more than a child myself, I found myself ministering to a mob of boys, age four to six, who ran like deer, cried like infants, fought like cats, and cursed like stevedores. My first day as their camp counselor was utter chaos, in part because the boys were all wearing their names pinned to their chests on fluttering paper, and the papers flew off in the brisk early summer wind, and the pins stuck the boys, and they stuck each other with the pins, etc. But things settled down over the next few days, and we became easy with one another, as easy as a coltish and dreamy teenager can be with a gaggle of boys mere months, in some cases, from toddlerhood.

There was David, who hardly spoke, and Daniel, who spoke for him and who wept when he soiled himself once, too frightened to tell me his pressing need. David told me about it, quietly, touching me on the shoulder, whispering, *Counselor, Danny needs you.* Daniel, five years old, was the first child I ever wiped clean, and I believe now that when we stood together in a sweltering dirty toilet on a July morning many years ago, Daniel sobbing compulsively as I washed him with a moist cloth, that we were engaged in a gentle sacrament: Daniel learning that he must confess to be cleansed, me understanding dimly that my silence with this weeping child was the first wise word I had ever spoken.

There was Anthony, a tough even then; and there were his running mates, brothers who guarded their real names and went by

Tom and Tim; and there was Lucius, a long lock of a boy, closed for repairs all that summer, unwilling to be touched, first to lash out. There was Miguel, age four physically, age fourteen emotionally, who fell in love with the ethereally lovely teenage girl who ran the arts-and-crafts room. Miguel came to me one rainy morning and asked, *Counselor, can you give me away?* I conducted negotiations, traded him, and saw him only occasionally the rest of the summer, usually trailing in the scented wake of his love, sucked along in her sweet eddy like a lifeboat trailing an exquisitely beautiful ocean liner. Although once, late in the afternoon, just as the buses were pulling away in pairs from the parking lot, I saw Miguel, alone, sitting in a front passenger seat, buckled in, hunched, sobbing; and for a moment, for all his eerie bravura, he was a baby again, frightened and bereft. I was not man enough myself then to go to him, and I drove away and left him in tears.

A sin: not my first, not my last.

There were Seth and Saul and Milton, who arrived together every morning in a large car driven by a silent man in a uniform, the boys spilling out of the car with gym bags intertwined like forest vines, the three of them inseparably tangled, yet apparently incapable of affection. They argued all day long in their shrill birdy voices, argued about balls and lanyards and swim trunks, about towels and mothers and thermos jugs, about sneakers and small gluey houses made of ice-cream sticks, argued all the way back to the elm tree where they waited late in the day for their driver, who never once opened his mouth, but drove up silently in the humming car, parked, emerged slowly from the front seat (unfolding himself in stages like an enormous jackknife), ushered the boys into the back seat (their thin sharp voices hammering away at each other like the jabs of featherweights), closed the back door (the camp air suddenly relieved of the shivered fragments of their tiny angers), plopped back into the front seat (the fat dark leather cushions exhaling sharply with a pneumatic hiss), and drove away (the long dark car dervishing the leaves of summer in its wake).

41

These then were the Meteorites, ten strong before we traded Miguel, nine strong on good days, that is to say the days when David's mother let him come to camp. She worried that he was autistic, which he was not, just quiet to the point of monastic silence, except when it came to jelly orgies, during which he howled as madly as his fellows as the jelly was cornered, slain, and gobbled raw. None of the Meteorites ate anything but jelly, sopping, dripping, quivering plates of it, attacked swiftly with white plastic spoons, the spoons clicking metronomically against their teeth, the vast cacophonous lunchroom filled to bursting with small sweating children shrieking and gulping down jelly as fast as they could get the shrieks out and the jelly in. In my first days in the jelly maelstrom, I raged at the boys as loudly as they howled at me; but by the end of the summer, I had learned to sit quietly and watch the waves of sound crash on the gooey tables, slide halfway up the long windows, and slowly recede.

Although I was by title a camp counselor, there was no camp at the camp, which was actually a vast estate owned by the town and rented out in the summer to an organization that offered the summer day-camp experience to children from three counties for six different fee scales, the lowest just manageable for poor and the highest enough to buy a car. The estate house itself was enormous, labyrinthine, falling apart, very nearly a castle in its huge architectural inexplicability. Its unkempt grounds sprawled for many acres of fields, forests, and glades. Beneath the honeycombed house ran a small-gauge railroad that the childless owner had built for his nieces and nephews: it consisted of three cars, each as big as a sofa, and an ingeniously laid track that slipped in and out of the house and hill like a sinuous animal. The cars and track were, of course, expressly forbidden to campers and counselors alike, and so, in the way of all things forbidden, they were mesmerizingly alluring and were filled every evening with counselors in various states of undress and inebriation.

But the counselors in the railroad cars at night were only a fraction of the counselors as a whole, for most of us drove off in the afternoon in the camp's buses, carting home our charges and returning them sticky and tired to their parents. The buses peeled away two by two, and when they were gone, the camp stood nearly silent in the long afternoon light. Bereft of the bustling populace of the day except, here and there in the forest fringes or sunning by the pool, a few counselors in entangled pairs. Once that summer I persuaded a friend to take my bus route, and I stayed at camp until dark. I clambered up the stairs inside the house as far as I could go, and then climbed out onto a roof and sat for hours, high above the oaks and maples, watching. I remember the long bars of slanting light, the sighing and snapping of the metal roof as it cooled from the roaring heat of the day, the soaring of a brown hawk over the farthest softball field, the burbling of three pigeons on a nearby roofline, the wriggles of marijuana smoke from the archery yard, the faint sounds of voices far below me, under the house, in the tunnels. When dusk came, I climbed down, leaving the roof to the pigeons. I could pick out the shapes of counselors against the hunched trees, some running, some walking arm-in-arm, the only lights in the thick grainy twilight the blazing ends of their cigarettes and joints, moving through the dark like meteorites. I found a friend and hitched a ride home.

The Meteorites and I were for the most part interested in the same things—games, balls, hawks, bones, food, trees, hats, buses, songs with snickered words about body functions, the girl who graced Miguel's dreams, and archery. They were absolutely obsessed with archery, although they could hardly handle even the tiniest bows, and even those bows mostly snapped emptily and whizzed over their ducking heads when they tried to draw back the strings, the arrows falling heavily to the ground without even a semblance of flight. When Meteorites ran away from the herd, which they did about once per week per boy, they could without fail be found in the archery alley, a broad grassy sward lined with stone walls and sheltered by sycamores whose fingers waved high above us and sent down shifting flitches of sunlight.

My great fear as counselor was that runaway boys would head either to the pool or through the woods to the highway, but they never did, not once. To the bows they went like arrows, and I would find them there a little later, watching the patient archery girl show them, for the hundredth time, how to grip the bow, how to notch the arrow to the string (the arrow shaking badly), how to pull the curve of the bow back to their sighting eye (their soprano grunts like the hoarse chuffing of pigeons as they hauled on the little bows with all the power they could muster), and how to loose the arrow with a flick of the fingers (a rain of bows in the air, a shower of arrows falling limply to the earth). At that point I would emerge from the sycamores and reclaim my Meteorite.

I don't remember that I ever scolded a runaway, for the archery girl was beautiful as well as gentle and the archery lane a tranquil island. Years later, when I read books about the Middle Ages in England and France, filled with castles and archery and knights and such, my mind reflexively set the action in that quiet green alley where bows flew and arrows lay facedown in the grass. For all the violence of the sharp arrows that did, on rare occasions, actually puncture the hay-stuffed targets, the archery lane was a wonderfully peaceful place, and my mind wanders back there even now, from the chaos and hubbub of my middle years.

The days of the Meteorites were circumscribed by geography. We were to be in certain places at certain times—the basketball court in the early morning (dew on the court, a toad or two), the arts-and-crafts room midmorning (Miguel's eyes riveted to the face of his beloved), the gym before lunch (the rubbery slam of dodgeballs against walls, the clatter of glasses flying to the floor when a small boy was hit full in the face), on the softball field after lunch (languid, hot, song of cicadas), the pool (shimmering and cool and perfect) and archery lane in midafternoon, the basketball court again late in the day. I was nominally the basketball teacher, and so conducted ragged drills and motley scrimmages not only for the Meteorites, some of whom were barely bigger than the ball, but also for young Comets, Planets, and Asteroids (known to the rest of the camp as Hemorrhoids). I also coached the older boys, who came to the court in increasingly insolent waves, ending with my last class of the day, the Seniors, sneeringly fourteen and fifteen years old, some as tan and strong as their teacher, and one— only one, always one—determined to defeat his teacher in pitched combat.

That one was Andy, Randy Andy, sniggering scourge of the Senior Girls, artfully tousled black hair and puka-shell necklace, quick fists and a switchblade carried for show. Andy stole a bus, stole money, groped girls, smoked dope, came to camp drunk, started a brushfire near the softball field, cursed the camp director, urinated on walls, crucified toads to trees, beat a smaller boy bloody, and, hours after striking out near the end of a counselors-Seniors softball game, carefully smashed all sixteen of the camp's bats to splinters—sizes 24 (Pee Wee Reese model) through 42 (Richie Allen model).

I have sometimes imagined the dark poetry of that act, the camp silent after hours, Andy emerging from his hiding place in the estate house, strolling down through the gathering dusk to the softball fields, dragging out the dusty canvas bat bag from the equipment shed, selecting the Pee Wee Reese model (you want to start small before working up to Dick Allen), taking a couple of practice cuts, selecting a young oak to absorb the blow in its belly, and then the sick crump of bat barrel against tree bone and the sudden green welt lashed oozing into the oak, and then a second swing and crack and shatter as the bat explodes. Andy drops the shaggy handle, shakes his hands to shuck the sting, and reaches for a 26: a Luis Aparicio. And through the thin woods the sound of vengeance echoes for almost an hour, until darkness.

Andy and I hated each other from the minute we met, as he slouched against a tree and muttered a joke under his breath while I explained a basketball drill to the restless Seniors. I was only a few years older than he was, and nervous, so I got in his face, and from that instant—a windy late afternoon in July, our faces an inch apart, his blackheads marching from one temple to another, my finger poking too hard into the little bowl of skin at the base of his throat—we were relentless enemies. It is a mark of my own chalky insecurity and mulish youth that I hounded Andy every chance I got, reporting his crimes to the director, ragging him from the sidelines of softball games, and once, by incredible luck, catching his fist in mid-swing (he was about to punch another boy for the second time) and so mortifying him before a girl, the ultimate humiliation for him and for me too, then. And now.

So every day at three o'clock, when the Seniors slouched up to my court and ran my drills and then circled watchfully as Andy and I stripped off our shirts to play one-on-one, there was the entrancing shock of possible blood in the air, and once there was blood in the air, mine. Andy waited patiently for the right long rebound and the right angle of me chasing it headlong, and as I lunged for the ball, he lashed his elbow into my mouth as hard as he could. But I won, and his hate rose another notch. I remember the garlic taste of my rage in my throat, and the tight circle of boys around us, staring, the only sounds the sharp shuffle of sneakers on dusty pavement and the relentless hammer of the ball.

Flirting with the female lifeguards was a nearly universal and daily habit among the hundreds of male creatures at the camp. It was a rare male counselor who did not detour his charges past the pool on their way to anywhere else. Not even the camp director, an ebullient and brilliant con man named Buck, was immune. He arranged his office in such a way that his gaze naturally strolled out the open French doors of the house veranda and down a short flight of stone steps to the pool. He spun on his huge chair, his eyes on the bikinis in the middle distance, recruiting students there is no camp on the entire North Shore that can offer the recreational and educational amenities we can, charming parents I understand that Marc has been named Camper of the Week three weeks running an unprecedented honor I may say and speaking of honor we would be honored to see you and Mr. Harrow at the annual Inner Circle dinner for special friends and benefactors, chasing delinquent fees I don't think you understand, Mrs. Kaplan, if we do not receive remuneration of your outstanding bill we will have to cancel Glen's pool privileges which will come as a terrible blow to the boy, evading creditors my accountant tells me that the check was delivered yesterday via registered mail, arguing with his wife you told the Kaufmans their twins could come free!?, flirting with his wife what say we knock off early and knock one off, checking his toupee in the mirror goddamned rugs, writing camp advertisements more than one hundred acres of fields and fun staffed by one hundred board-certified educators, badgering food and gasoline and sports equipment and T-shirt vendors yes, sixteen bats, various weights, and placating angry parents I can assure you Mrs. Steinberg that David's counselor was with him from the minute the accident occurred until his arrival at the oral surgeon's office, and that this young fellow, a Cornell University engineering student I might add, had foresightedly brought both of David's teeth with him in the ambulance. At every possible opportunity, Buck sauntered down to the pool, ostensibly to check on the insurance, the floats, the filter, the schedule, but really to savor the lithe bodies of his female employees. Because the camp sat high on a windy hill not far from the ocean, it was cold in the morning, even in July and August, and the lifeguards wore their sweatsuits until noon or so. After a few weeks I noticed that Buck conducted all his business in the morning so that he could be at the pool in the afternoon. When the sweatsuits were off.

The geometric light of high summer, the smell of chlorine, the shouts of children in the shallow end, the cannonball geysers of older boys hurtling into the middle by the bobbined rope, the streaming hair of Senior girls emerging blinking from the deep end, I remember it all now, my mind back in the itchy young cat-body I had then. I am bouncing down the stone steps toward the pool, peeling off my wet shirt, one eye on the shambling parade of Meteorites behind me watch the steps gentlemen the steps, the other eye staring at the shadow between the breasts of a girl in a bright yellow bikini fifty feet away. I take the last four steps in a casual easy bound and then lean easily into the pool, shorts and socks and sneakers and all, and as I go under I can hear the high-pitched voices of my boys in wild amazement: *Counselor went in with his sneakers on...!*

Of course I fell in love that summer, led there by the Meteorites. For weeks they watched me stare helplessly at one of the lifeguards, a shy lovely girl, and then one day they somehow conspired among themselves to bring her to me. They led her by the hand up the rickety stone steps of the castle, up the balustrade, down a wooden hall lined with sagging metal lockers, to our locker room, lined with sagging benches. I was slumped in the corner, adjusting the bandana I wore all that summer, waiting impatiently for the boys to change into their bathing trunks, their thin white slippery bodies like the startling white roots of plants just pulled from the ground. In walked Nancy, in her bathing suit. She was flanked by David and Daniel, who led her toward me by the hand, and then stepped back, Daniel giggling, David not.

I was very startled. There are few moments in life when you are idly dreaming about a book, a place, a meal, a girl, and you look up and there is your dream before you. Her hair was drying at the ends but still wet and tight to her head; one foot rested on the other as she leaned against a locker. Daniel was dancing about like an elf, quite proud of himself, but David was staring at me, waiting for something: a look I would not again see for years, until one of my own children, at the same age, regarded me as soberly with such powerful expectation.

Please sit down, here, sit here, move over Lucius, I say.

Lucius glares.

I'm so seeprised to sue you here, I say.

The boys giggle at my tangled tongue.

The boys told me you liked me very much, she says.

My God.

And I like you, she says. Very much.

My God.

I, I've liked you for a long time, I say.

And with that we rose, as if rising simultaneously was what we had in mind, as if we had agreed on something. We collected the boys (Tim was hiding behind the locker naked), and we paraded the Meteorites down the rickety stairs and toward the pool. Somewhere on the stairs we held hands, and so began that summer love, doomed and perfect, having much to do with the taste of sunburned skin, car radios, bitter words on lawns, letters on looseleaf paper, bright yellow notes on the driver's seat of my bus at dusk, her college boyfriend, her coy best friend, her mother's sharp eyes, the door of her room half-open, her shirt half-off, her face half-turned away.

The Meteorites are in their mid-twenties now, college graduates mostly, I would guess, and at work, married, in prison, who knows? I have thought about them every summer—summer brings me the Meteorites, ten strong always, Miguel still one of us—but I have never made the slightest effort to see them again. They would not remember me, and in their rangy men's bodies, long-boned, tending to first fat, I would not recognize the four- and five- and six-year-olds they were. Yet I think of them more every year. I have small children of my own now, and I am surrounded again by hubbub and jelly; and it is summer as I write, with the smell of hot afternoon on my shirt.

But there is more than memory here, more than nostalgia, more than a man's occasional yearning to be the quick boy he was. I learned about love, how to love, that summer—and not from the girl who came from the water, although I loved her and she me, for a time. No, I loved David because he loved Daniel; because David came to me that August morning and touched me on the shoulder and whispered, *Counselor, Danny needs you*; because after I cleaned Daniel, in that filthy bathroom, David was waiting, his glasses askew, and when Daniel and I emerged into the clean sunshine, the boys embraced each other, their thin fluttering hands like birds on the bones of their shoulders.

Counselor, Danny needs you, spoken by a small boy on a high hill, and the four words fell from his mouth and were scattered by the four winds, years ago: but they have been a storm in me.

First Kiss

One thing no one informs you of when you get ready to kiss a girl
For the first time is where to put your nose: do you lay it alongside
Hers, like a skipper eases his ship along a dock, or do you take turns,
Alternating left and right? You laugh, but this is a pressing question,
As you well remember yourself. And your hands—do they...quest?
Or do they alight on her shoulders like birds, like leaves? The glasses
On each of your noses—is it sweet when they clink, or is that dorkish?
Should you take them off just before you kiss, or is that too confident
That you will be kissing? And most of all the breathing. This is a real
Problem. Do you hold your breath? Do you aim for staggered breaths
Like in the pool? And who is in charge? If your partner wants to retire,
What are the accepted signal flags for such a decision? Can I appeal?
I hear you laughing, but you were in the same boat. We were shaking.
We so wanted to do this well and so wanted not to be seen to want to.
In a sense it was practice for so very many things that we would want
But would not know how to get, or know what to do with after we got
Them. You know full well what I mean. Nothing was as gently sweet,
Nothing so roaringly nerve-racking; how could both things be true at
Once? How could that be? Yet it was so, and would be hourly more so.

[Silence]

For several days when we were young, my sister stayed silent. She was perhaps twenty, a student of spirituality. I was thirteen, a student of surliness. She announced that she would be silent for a while and then commenced to be so. My parents were gracious about it. Seems like there's a lot more room in the house now, said my dad. We should applaud and celebrate this form of prayer, said my mom. *Cooool,* my brothers said. Is this permanent?

Eventually my sister spoke again—to yell at me, as I recall—but I never forgot those days. I was reminded of it recently when she emerged from a very long silence at the Buddhist monastery where she now lives, and I asked her what her first words were when she emerged from her silent retreat, and she grinned and said, "Pass the butter," which I did, which made her laugh, because those actually were her first words after the retreat.

I *really* wanted that butter, she says.

Is it hard to be silent? I ask.

In the beginning it is, she says. Then it becomes a prayer.

I contemplate snippets of silence in mine existence and find them few; but I find that this delights rather than dismays me, for the chaos and hubbub in my life, most of my sea of sound, are my children, who are small quicksilver russet testy touchy tempestuous mammals always underfoot in the understory, yowling and howling and weeping and chirping and teasing and shouting and moaning and laughing and singing and screaming and sneering and sassing and humming and snoring and wheezing and growling and muttering and mumbling and musing and so making magic music all the livelong day. Which is pretty cool; though it will not be permanent.

But sometimes they are silent and I am a student of their silence: my teenage daughter absorbed in book or homework, curled in her chair like a cat in the thicket of her room; my sons asleep, their limbs flung to the four holy directions, their faces beatific, their bedclothes rippled hills and dells, their beds aswarm with socks and shirts and books and balls; or all three children dozing in the back seat of the car as we slide through the velvet night, their faces flashing cinematically in my mirror as streetlights snick by metronomically; or the way they sat together silently before the silent television one crystal morning, four years ago, and watched two flaming towers crumble down down down unto unthinkable unimaginable ash and dust. Silently the towers fell, and silently my children watched, the twin scars burning into their brains.

I ask my sister questions:

What did you do when you were silent?

I *listened,* she says. I listened really hard.

Did you make any noise at all?

Sometimes I found myself humming, she says, but it wasn't any music I'd known before. Which is pretty interesting. Where does music come from that you never heard before?

Good question, I say.

And I found, she says, that it is relatively easy not to talk to other people, but much harder not to talk to animals. Isn't that odd? Why would that be?

Another good question, I say.

We had peacocks and guinea fowl at the monastery, she says, and I was sort of in charge of the birds, which we had for two reasons. The peacocks someone gave us, which we thought was a generous if unusual gift until we had them for a while, and we realized what loud vain foul mean evil creatures they are, at which point we all thought, *What sort of sick human being would deliberately* give *a peacock to another human being?* It's a *punishment* to have peacocks around, they peck and screech at you and make your life miserable, but the guinea fowl, now, they're not mean, no, that's not their problem, their problem is that they are without doubt or debate the most unbelievably stupid creatures ever to walk the earth, so incredibly stupid that you wonder how in heaven's name they ever managed to survive as a species, and the times I really *really* wanted to talk had to do with those guinea fowl, who were so mindbogglingly stupid I wanted to shriek. I mean, if they were three feet away from the henhouse, and somehow got turned around so they were facing away from the henhouse, well, rather than have the inclination or imagination to turn back around, they'd stand there sobbing and wailing, as if utterly lost in the wilderness. Ye gods. You'd have to physically pick them up and turn them around toward the henhouse. You could almost see the delight on their faces as the henhouse reappeared. *There it is again! It's a miracle!* Ye gods.

Let us consider silence as destination, ambition, maturity of mind, focusing device, filter, prism, compass point, necessary refuge, spiritual refreshment, touchstone, lodestar, home, natural and normal state in which let's face it we began our existence in the warm seas of our mothers, all those months when we did not speak, and swam in salt, and dreamed oceanic dreams, and heard the throb and hum of mother, and the murmur and mutter of father, and the distant thrum of a million musics waiting patiently for you to be born.

I rise early and apply myself to my daily reading. Herman Melville: *All profound things and emotions of things are preceded and amended by Silence, and Silence is the general consecration of the universe.* Thomas Merton: *A man who loves God necessarily loves silence.* Jorge Luis Borges: *Absolute silence is the creative energy and intelligence of eternal being.* Book of Job: *I put my finger to my lips and I will not answer again.* Melville once more, poetically pithy in the midst of the vast sea of his sentences: *Silence is the only Voice of our God.*

To which I can only say (silently): amen.

It's harder to be silent in summer than in winter, says my sister. It's harder to be silent in the afternoon than in the morning. It's hardest to be silent when eating with others. It's easy to be silent in the bath. It's easy to be silent in the bed. It's easiest to be silent near water, and easiest of all to be silent by the lips of rivers and seas.

The silence of chapels and churches and confessionals and glades and gorges, places that wait for words to be spoken in the caves of their ribs. The split second of silence before two people simultaneously burst into laughter. The pregnant pause. The hot silence of lovemaking. The stifling stifled brooding silence just before a thunderstorm unleashes itself wild on the world. The silence of space, the vast of vista. The crucial silences between notes, without which there could be no music; no yes without no.

I study the silence of my wife. Her silence when upset; a silence I hear all too well after twenty years of listening for it. Her riveted silence in chapel. Her silence rocking children all those thousands of hours in the dark, the curved maple chair murmuring, hum of the heater, rustle of fevered boy resting against the skin of the sea from which he came.

My sister was loud as a teenager, cigarettes and music and shrieking at her brothers, but she gentled as the years went by, and much of my memory of her has to do with her sitting at the table with my mother, the two women talking quietly, the swirl of cigarette smoke circling, their voices quick and amused and circling, the mind of the mother circling the mind of the daughter and vice versa, a form of play, a form of love, a form of literature.

I rise earlier and earlier in these years. I don't know why. Age, sadness, a willingness to epiphany. Something is opening in me, some new eye.

I talk less and listen more. Stories wash over me all day like tides. I walk through the bright wet streets and every moment a story comes to me, people hold them out to me like sweet children, and I hold them squirming and holy in my arms, and they enter my heart for a while, and season and salt sweeten that old halting engine and teach me humility and mercy, the only lessons that matter, the lessons of the language I most wish to learn; a tongue best spoken without a word, without a sound, hands clasped, heart naked as a baby.

The Final Frontier

It is the rare soul who remembers particular lines from Scripture for reasons other than professional advancement or private absorption. But I remember, even as a child, being totally riveted by certain odder blunter saltier lines that made me elbow my wry patient dad, like *be kind to your father even when his mind goes,* or the ones where the Christos isn't so much godlike as he is a rattled guy, such as when he whirls and shouts *who touched my clothes?!,* after he *felt the power leave him,* what a phrase!

One of those lines for me has always been *blessed are the poor in spirit.* I heard it for the first time as a child, of course, at Mass, late in the morning, drowsing between my alpine dad and willowy mother, in a pew filled with brothers seated with parental buffers so as to reduce fisticuffery, and like everyone else I was puzzled and nonplussed. Wasn't the whole point to be *rich* in spirit? How could you be bereft spirit-wise but get a backstage pass to the Kingdom of Heaven? What was *that* about? Was it a major serious printer's error no one had noticed all these years? Was it supposed to be *pear* in spirit, or something artsy like that?

Diligent schoolteachers subsequently explained the phrase to me, and my gentle wise parents explained it, and learned university professors explained it, and able scholarly writers explained it, and I got the general idea, that the word *poor* there is better understood as *humble,* but *humble* never really registered for me because I was *not* humble, and had no real concept of humble, until my wife married me, which taught me a shocking amount about humility, and then we were graced by children, which taught me a *stunning* amount about humility, and then friends of mine began to wither and shrivel and die in all sorts of ways including being roasted to death on September 11th and I began, slowly and dimly, to realize that humble was the only finally truly honest way to be in this life. Anything else is ultimately cocky, which is either foolish or a deliberate disguise you refuse to remove, for complicated reasons perhaps not known even to you.

Of course you do your absolute best to find and hone and wield your divine gifts against the dark. You do your best to reach out tenderly to touch and elevate as many people as you can reach. You bring your naked love and defiant courage and salty grace to bear as much as you can, with all the attentiveness and humor you can muster. This life is after all a miracle and we ought to pay fierce attention every moment, as much as possible.

But you cannot control anything. You cannot order or command everything. You cannot fix and repair everything. You cannot protect your children from pain and loss and tragedy and illness. You cannot be sure that you will always be married, let alone happily married. You cannot be sure you will always be employed, or healthy, or relatively sane.

All you can do is face the world with quiet grace and hope you make a sliver of difference. Humility does not mean self-abnegation, lassitude, detachment; it's more a calm recognition that you must trust in that which does not make sense, that which is unreasonable, illogical, silly, ridiculous, crazy by the measure of most of our culture. You must trust that you being the best possible you matters somehow. That trying to be an honest and tender parent will echo for centuries through your tribe. That doing your chosen work with creativity and diligence will shiver people far beyond your ken. That being an attentive and generous friend and citizen will prevent a thread or two of the social fabric from unraveling. And you must do all of this with the certain knowledge that you will never get proper credit for it, and in fact the vast majority of things you do right will go utterly unremarked. *Humility, the final frontier,* as my brother Kevin used to say. When we are young we build a self, a persona, a story in which to reside, or several selves in succession, or several at once, sometimes; when we are older we take on other roles and personas, other masks and duties; and you and I both know men and women who become trapped in the selves they worked so hard to build, so desperately imprisoned that sometimes they smash their lives simply to escape who they no longer wish to be; but finally, I think, if we are lucky, if we read the book of pain and loss with humility, we realize that we are all broken and small and brief, that none among us is ultimately more valuable or rich or famous or beautiful than another; and then, perhaps, we begin to understand something deep and true about humility.

This is what I know: that the small is huge, that the tiny is vast, that pain is part and parcel of the gift of joy, and that this is love, and then there is everything else. You either walk toward love or away from it with every breath you draw. Humility is the road to love. Humility, maybe, *is* love. That could be. *I* wouldn't know; I'm a muddle and a conundrum shuffling slowly along the road, gaping in wonder, trying to just see and say what is, trying to leave shreds and shards of ego along the road like wisps of litter and chaff.

Jones Beach

At the beach, many years ago with my family, bitten by the wind,
Pebbled by whipping sand, my sister older and remote and fifteen,
My mother leery of the water, my dad as usual calm and dignified
Though hilariously and uncharacteristically wearing swimming trunks,
The sandwiches gritty, the grapes sugared by sand, our cookie bits
Drawing gangs of grim seagulls, the people of every color swirling
Around us, their musical incomprehensible imprecations and radio
Stations, a man drowns; there is a shrill and a blare and a lifeguard
Brown as dusk sprints like a fullback through the whirling children
Along the murmuring shore his brilliant float trailing him like a sin.
A few moments later they hauled in the dead man mottled and blue
And that was that. I remember there was a man selling beer and ice
That day, walking through the crowd, wary of the beach patrol cop.
I remember burly boys diving into the relentless surf after footballs.
I remember terns whiter than white cut against blue sharp as knives.
I remember my youngest brother weeping, his face masked by sand.
Late in the afternoon it grew cold and we packed up and went home.
I remember the sand in the car, the grizzled salt of my dad's haircut.
We regret what we forget but we remember far more than we forget:
We forget that. Once a man sold beer and ice; another drank the sea.
My mother wore a green suit. There were beautiful girls by the jetty.

The Wonder of the Look on Her Face

Iwas in an old wooden church recently, way up in the north country, and by chance I got to talking to a girl who told me she was almost nine years old. The way she said it, you could hear the opening capital letters on the words *Almost* and *Nine*. She had many questions for me. Did I know the end of my stories before I wrote them? Did my stories come to me in dreams? Her stories came to her in dreams. Did the talking crow in one of my books go to crow school? Where did crows have their schools? Did the crow's friends talk, too? Did they have jokes that only crows know? Did I write with a typewriter like her grandfather? Did I use a computer? If you write on a computer, do the words have electricity in them? Is it too easy to write on a computer? Do you write better if you write slower? She wrote with a pencil. She was about to start writing her third book. Her first book was about bears, and her second book was about her grandfather's fishing boat. Her grandfather still owned the boat even though he was too old to go fishing. He would go sit in the boat sometimes when it was at the dock, though. It took him a long time to get into and out of the boat, but he wouldn't let anyone help him in and out of the boat because he was a Mule-Headed Man. He let a young man go fishing in the boat, though. The young man wanted to buy the boat, but her grandfather wouldn't sell it no matter what. So the young man paid her grand-father in money and fish he caught when he used the boat. Her family ate an awful lot of fish sometimes. She thought her third book was go-ing to be about a mink. She wasn't sure yet. Could you write a book if you didn't know what would happen in it? I said yes, you could. I said that, in fact, it seemed to me that the writing was a lot more fun if you were regularly surprised and startled and even stunned by what happened. I said that maybe one way to write a good book was to just show up ready to listen to the people and animals and trees in the book, and write down what they said and did. I said that I supposed you could know everything that was going to happen, and even draw yourself a map of what should happen, and then try hard to make that happen, but that didn't seem as much fun as having a rough idea of what might happen and then being startled quite often by what did happen. I said that I rather enjoyed that the people and animals in my books didn't listen too much to what I thought should happen, hard as it was sometimes for me to watch. I said that I wasn't saying one way was better than another way, and that probably you could write good books in all sorts of ways, certainly I was not particularly wise about how to write good books, because I wrote only one book at a time, and very slowly, too, and whatever I learned while writing one book seemed to be utterly lost the next time I wrote a book, because the books were as different as people or animals or trees are, and whatever you think you know about a person or an animal or a tree because it is a certain species or color or nativity is probably egregiously wrong, because assumptions are foolish, as far as I could tell. She said that one of her ambitions was to someday write a book with a really good pen, and I said that, by happy chance, I had a terrific pen on my person, in the shirt pocket where I always carry pens with which to start books if book-starting seems necessary, and that one thing authors should be with each other is generous with good pens. So I gave her my pen, observing that it might have a very good book in it, especially if the book was about minks, or otters, which are fascinating animals, as everyone knows. She accepted the pen gingerly, with great care, with a look on her face that I wish I could express in words. But even excellent words like *astonishment* and *joy* and *gravity* and *awe* and *reverence* do not quite catch the wonder of the look on her face.

The Old Typewriter in the Basement

Once again a student asks me how I became a writer, and this time I say, Because of the staccato staggered music of my dad's old typewriter in the basement. Because when he really got it going you could listen to it like a song. Because after a while you could tell if he was writing a book review or a letter just from the shift and drift of the thrum of the thing. Because it sounded cheerful and businesslike and efficient and workmanlike and true. Because a bell rang when he came to the end of a line, and you could hear him roll sheets of paper in and out of the carriage, and you could imagine him carefully lining up the carbon sheet to the face sheet, and he typed with two fingers faster than anyone we knew could type with ten, and he had the professional journalist's firm confident knowledgeable hammer-stroke with those forefingers, as if those fingers knew perfectly well what they wanted to say and were going about their business with a calm alacrity that you could listen to all day long. Because his typewriter had dozens of deft machined metal parts and they had cool names like *spool* and *platen* and *ribbon*. Because his typewriter was a tall old typewriter that he loved and kept using even when electric typewriters hove into view and tried to vibrate onto his desk. Because if you stared closely at the keys, as I did quite often, you could see which letters he used more than other letters. Because the typewriter was him and he was our hero and we loved him and we wanted to be like him which is why we all learned to type. Because you would daydream of writing a story on his typewriter but you would never actually do so because using his typewriter would be like driving God's car. Because his typewriter stood proudly in the center of his desk and there were books and magazines and dictionaries and neat stacks of paper and manila folders and newspaper clippings and rulers and erasers and pencils and pens and a jar of rubber cement and not one but two X-acto knives sharper than a falcon's talons, and above his desk was a shelf crowded with dictionaries and catechisms and manuals and other books of all sorts, many of them bristling with bookmarks and scraps of paper marking particular pages or passages of heft and verve and dash and wit. Because when he went downstairs to his desk you could be in any room upstairs even unto the attic and hear the first hesitant strokes as he began typing, and then the sprint and rattle and rollick as he hit his stride, and then an impossibly short pause between the end of one page and the start of another, a break so brief that you could not believe he could whip one sheet out and whirl another in so fast unless you saw it with your own eyes which we did sometimes peeking from the door of the study into which no child was allowed when Dad was typing for fear you would interrupt his thoughts which were no kidding Putting Food on the Table, you will not under any circumstances interrupt your father when he is in his study, if you are bleeding come upstairs and bleed, and inform me of the cause of bleeding, and if you cannot find me find your sister, and if you cannot find either of us stanch the bleeding with a hand-towel, not a bath-towel, and go next door and ask the neighbors for assistance if necessary. Because he had been typing since he was a boy, and because all the love letters he wrote to our mother when he was far away deep in the tropics in the war were meticulously typed, and the poems he sent were meticulously typed, and because he told me once that he had several times in his thirties tried to rise before dawn to type a novel, even as the house was filled with small children and he was due on the early train to his press job in the city, but he did not have the energy to invent and embroider, and he would fall asleep with his head in his arms on the typewriter, and startle awake after a while, and never finish his novels. But I have written novels, and there are times, many times, when

I think that I have done so in large part because of him and his old typewriter and the sound of his cheerful efficient staccato typing in the basement. Because he is still our hero and we love him and we want to be like him more than ever. Because maybe my novels are somehow the novels he started to write and could not finish. Perhaps somehow I have finished them for him and he startles awake and grins ruefully at his old typewriter and pads upstairs to wake the kids and I am typing these last words with my forefingers and with tears sliding slowly into my beard.

The Old Methodist Church
on Vashon Island

I read aloud from my headlong prose the other night
In a gentle old wooden church on an island and then
People wanted me to sign books and such but I have
Learned that mostly they do not want my scribble as
Much as they want to *say* something to me. So often
What they have to say is quiet and haunting and just
Enough of their deepest self that you both just stand
There startled and quiet for an instant with that story
Between you like it slid out without any forethought;
A sort of jailbreak where you cannot believe you've
Actually made it outside the walls. So this happened,
And I stood there with this guy and his long-lost son,
And neither of us said a word, and I bet we stood for
A minute with the boy between us. He would be five
Years old now, and he would be sleepy, and I would
Goof him and ask him if he was going to have a beer
Before he went to bed and he would shyly say nooo!,
And we would all smile and then his dad would sling
Him on his shoulder and he and I would shake hands,
The dad using his left hand so he didn't drop the boy,
And I would turn politely to the next reader and offer
To deface their book. I guess what I wanted to say to

You here is that this did not happen but it did happen.
For a moment there was the little boy behind his dad,
Shy and sleepy and clutching his dad's Sunday pants.
For a minute there was a kid who was and isn't but is.

III.

We Can Take Off Our
Masks, or, If We Can't Do
That, We Can Squawk
Through the Holes in
Them. A Squawk Is Better
Than Nothing

Testimonio

Iwas at a conference the other day, and there was a reception, and people were making small talk, and I was happily babbling about sports, because one advantage to being a guy is that almost all guys are aware of sports and have an opinion or affiliation or affection or detestation of some team or sport or player thereof, when somehow the conversation swung to politics, which is dangerous ground because people get heated without having the slightest grip on fact, and one guy, why is it always a guy, started sneering courteously about someone else's opinion, and I made a joke to decaffeinate his sneer, and he sneered slightly too politely that humor is the refuge of cowards, and a synapse popped in my brain, and I delivered a speech that went something like this: Really? So Mark Twain was a coward? And Will Rogers and Robin Williams and the Dalai Lama and Desmond Tutu were cowards? Bob Hope, who visited a million soldiers where they were huddled under bullets and rockets and mortars and mud and fear, he was a coward? Jesus, with His wry puzzling conundrum remarks, He was a coward? People who try to deflect and defuse moments pregnant with blood and bruises and death are cowards? Is that so? People who use their brains to figure out ways around fists and sticks and iron pipes and knives and guns are cowards? People who get it that we are issued imagination in order to invent new ways to be, other than the old ways where the biggest most sociopathic among us snatched whatever and whoever they wanted, those people are cowards? People who make other people laugh, during which time no one is raped or beaten or imprisoned, those people are cowards? People who consciously and deliberately and with cheerful intent make other people laugh, so that everyone cools out and people start to drop their masks and disguises and defenses and personas and assumptions, those people are cowards? People who foment laughter, knowing that laughter actually no kidding drops blood pressure, and warms up rooms, and urges wallflowers an inch or two away from the wall, those people are cowards? Define *coward* for me, if you will, because you have me confused and puzzled here about what is cowardly and what is brave. Does *brave* mean *bloody* to you? So the antithesis of coward is someone who heats things up, pushes people closer to the wall, elevates their anger, forces masks and disguises and defenses back on tighter than before, that guy is not a coward? Is that right? Because I think a guy who sneers is an arrogant pompous self-absorbed ass, and I think that humor is a great weapon against that sort of arrogance, and I think that arrogance so very often leads to violence, and I think the worst slimy murderers in history were all arrogant pompous fatheads who were convinced that they knew best, and they were the smartest guys in the room, and whatever twisted vision they had of the world and its future was the only right and true one, and they are all roasting in the lowest cellars in hell, and everyone roasting down there with them has one thing in common, a preening sneering narcissistic arrogance that polluted the world for exactly as long as they were allowed to foul it with their presence in this life. Am I making myself clear? Is there any other prim stupid sneering thing you want to say at this juncture? Because I think we have come to the point in this conversation where small talk just scuttled off hurriedly into the distance, and it's time for you to stride off angrily, or time for us all to start telling entertaining stories in order to see under our masks and maybe get to some common ground in the few minutes we have before the next panel session begins. No cutting remark, to get your sneer back on? No? Good. I'll start—the eight stupidest things I have ever done in this life, in order, are...

Mea Culpa

Ilaughed at gay people. I did. I snickered at their crew cuts and sashay and flagrancy. I snickered at the way they bristled about their rights. I did. I accused them of inventing disco. I laughed at their thing for feathers and glitter and fragrance and form-fitting uniforms. I grinned at the epic extravagance of gay-pride parades. I laughed at the idea of gay guys battling cops hand-to-hand at Stonewall, noting that *that* must have been a brief battle. Then I began to stop being such a meathead. Perhaps it was the sight of people weeping over the withering of those they loved with all their hearts and souls that snapped me awake. I stopped laughing. I started weeping too. The first time I saw the quilt I wept. The quilt is the biggest quilt you ever saw. It is more than a million square feet big. It is haunting and beautiful and terrible and lovely and bright and awful. Every panel is someone who died young. Every panel has tears in it. There are more tears in the quilt than there are threads. I started paying attention. I started listening. I stopped sneering and snickering. I began to hear the pummel of blows rained down on people for merely being who they are. How different is that from skin color and religion and ethnicity and nationality and the language that you speak? It is no different. I started listening. I heard stridency and silly demands and self-absorption and prickly neurosis but I also heard honesty and love and sense and logic and reason. If all men are created equal, why do we not act that way? If all women are created equal, why do we not act that way? If someone loves someone else, what do I care what gender or orientation or identity they choose? If they want to be married to each other and enter the deeper confusing thorny wilderness of marriage, what do I care? The marriage of gay people is a slippery slope to what, exactly? *More* committed love? Is that a bad thing? Is it a bad thing that couples wish to care for children when more children than ever before are without two parents? How exactly is that a bad thing? Aren't two moms better than one? Who cares what gender the parents are? Isn't love bigger than gender? Also some people, a lot more than you would think, feel like they are born with the wrong body, and they switch bodies, and as far as I can tell they generally then are thrilled and comfortable and satisfied with their new bodies, and what do I care? This happened to a friend of mine, who spent thirty years as a man and then switched teams, and she has been a woman for fifty years, and you never met a more brilliant, generous, witty, gentle, wise, courteous, erudite, positive soul in your life. What is it exactly that is objectionable about her decision about her life? What do I care? What do *we* care? Where is there anything political in her decision? What sort of cold cruel arrogant religion would pronounce her decision sinful? Do not religions advocate love and mercy as the essential virtues? I have stopped sneering and snickering and laughing and teasing and making snide jokes about crew cuts and tight clothes and earrings. I was a fool. I was myself a joke, and not a good one. I said the words *mercy* and *love* and *attentiveness* and *humility* and *tolerance* and they were empty withered things in my mouth. No more. I am not gay. I am not bisexual. I am not lesbian. I am not transgender. I am not questioning. I am generally delighted and thrilled and comfortable and deeply satisfied with my body and my gender and my identity, except for some disconcerting spinal issues. But I no longer think that my body type and gender and identity give me license to sneer at other types. I never thought being a pale brown color gave me license to sneer at people who were russet or bronze or copper or taupe or ebony in color. I never thought that being male gave me license to sneer at people who were female. I stopped thinking that not being gay gives me license to sneer at people who are gay. It took me longer than it should have to stop thinking that, for which I apologize here in the last line of this essay. I have done many foolish things in this life, so far, and that was one of the most foolish, and cruel, and sinful. *Mea culpa. Mea maxima culpa.* Never again.

Yes

Lately I have been delving into early Irish literature and language, and so have been raiding cattle in Cuailnge, and pondering the visions of Oenghus, and feasting at Bricriu, and wooing Etain, which last has led to some tension with my wife, who is of Belgian extraction and does not like to hear me tell of the beautiful Etain, the loveliest woman in all Ireland, although Etain was changed to an insect and banished for a thousand years, until she was reborn as the wife of Eochaid Airem, king of the green lands.

I try to explain to my wife that I am wooing only by proxy, as it were, and that Eochaid has the inside track, he being in the story and me only reading it. This line of talk leads me inevitably to Flann O'Brien and Myles na gCopaleen and Brian O'Nolan, all of whom I wheel into the conversation, the three men standing all in the same spot, as if they were the same man, which they were, except when O'Nolan was writing, which is when he became one of the others depending on what he was writing—novels as O'Brien, journalism as na gCopaleen ("of the little horses") or sometimes Count O'Blather, or James Doe, or Brother Barnabas, or George Knowall.

My wife is unmoved; she will not have Etain in the house.

After a while I realize that the problem is the word *woo. It is a word that may be applied to your wife and your wife only, if you have a wife,* she is saying without saying. She is a subtle woman, which is part of the reason I wooed her years ago, and won her from various rivals, who did not woo so well, and went away, one may say, full of rue.

I spent some time after that saying *woo,* which is a very fine word, rife with meaning, and emitted with a lift from the lips, like *whee* and *who,* or *no.* By chance I happened to be saying *woo* in the presence of my new son Joseph, a curious young man three months of age. Like his father he is intrigued by sounds, and soon enough he too was saying *woo,* and then my other new son Liam, also three months old, picked it up, and the three of us were *woo*ing to beat the band, although then Liam burst into tears, and had to be carried away to another room for milk.

Joe and I kept it up, though; he is an indefatigable fellow. After a while he switched to *who,* and I went with him, to see where this would go, and it went back and forth between us for a while, and then it went to *whee,* and then back to *woo,* and then my wife came back in the room and found us *woo*ing like crazy men. By then it was Joe's turn for a suckle and off he went, and I went downstairs to raid cattle in Cuailnge, and ponder Oenghus, and feast at Bricriu, and woo Etain, of whom the less said the better.

The wooing of Etain demands a certain familiarity with the Gaelic tongue, which has fascinated me since I was a boy in my grandmother's lap listening to the swell and swing of Irish from her lips, which more often than you might expect had Gaelic oaths on them, as she was a shy woman with a sharp temper, though gentle as the night is long, and much mourned by many to this day. I still hear her voice on windy nights, banshee nights, saying to me, gently, *bí I do bhuachaill maith,* be a good boy, or *Go mbeannaí Dia thú,* God bless you. So partly in memory of my grandmother, a McCluskey before she was a Clancey giving her daughter to a Doyle, I have been marching through the thickets of the Irish tongue, the second oldest in Europe behind Basque, and the cold hard fact is that the Gaelic language is a most confusing creature, and although I don't understand very much of it I read about it at every opportunity, and have been able to note several interesting observations on small scraps of paper, which are then distributed willy-nilly in various pants pockets, emerging here and there like crumpled fish, and reminding me that I had meant to write an essay on the topic at, or more accurately in, hand.

Thus this story, which was supposed to be about the fact that there is no way to say the words *yes* and *no* in Gaelic, but swerved unaccountably into a disquisition about sounds, of which some are exuberant, like Joe's *woo,* and some affirmative, like *sea,* which is Gaelic for *it is,* and *yes* and *si* and *ja* and *oui,* which are English and Spanish and German and French for *yes,* which there is no way to say in Gaelic, try as you might.

Is it sayable in the Irish?

Nil—it is not.

Nil is as fascinating as *sea* to me, especially so lately because my daughter, Lily, a rebellious angel, age three, is fixated on *no,* which she says often, in different accents, with various degrees of vehemence. She says it morning, noon, and night, particularly at night, when she wakes up screaming *no no no no no,* and answers *nooooo* when I ask what is the matter. Sometimes she says *neuwh,* which is a sort of *no,* which is said usually after she has been watching Mary Poppins and is afflicted with a sort of stiffening of the upper lip which prevents proper pronunciation of simple words like *no.* It is interesting that she is riveted by *no* because her brother Liam is riveted by *ho,* which is the only word he owns at the moment. Like a geyser he emits *ho!* regularly and then subsides. I expect him to pick up *no* pretty soon, his sister being a whiz at it and the boys certain to learn at her knee, and then Joe will get *no* too and then my children will be saying *no* to beat the band, not to mention the thin stretched rubber of their father's patience which they hammer upon like a bodhran, the wee drum of my Wicklow ancestors.

But their father is in the basement at the moment musing over the fact that Gaelic always uses *tu,* or thou, when speaking to one person, or *sibh,* you, for more than one, which habit, he thinks, reflects a certain native friendliness in the tongue and in its speakers; and he further puzzles over the fact that Irish counts in twenties, not tens; and further he muses that Gaelic, at least in Ireland, has no terms for the *Mister* and *Señor* and *Herr* that English and Spanish and German use as terms of bourgeois respect, which makes him wonder about Irish independence as well as rural isolation. Also he spends a good deal of time pondering ogham, the alphabet used in Ireland for writing on wood and stone before the year 500 or so, when Christianity and the Latin alphabet rode into Ireland together on strong winds, and the fact that Gaelic has perhaps sixty phonemes, which are sounds that convey meaning, and of which there are perhaps forty-four in English, which comparative fact makes him wonder about the width of the respective languages, so to speak, which width is also reflected in the simple spelling and pronunciation of terms in each tongue: I might say of Liam that he is *an buachaill,* the boy, for example, and roll the former off my tongue and pop the latter out rather like *ho,* which is what Liam is saying as I am calling him *an buachaill.*

Further, I am fascinated by the fact that Gaelic is a language in love with nouns, as can be seen with a phrase that often occurs to me when I think about my daughter's and my sons' futures, *tá eagla orm,* which in English would be *I fear* but in Gaelic is *fear is upon me,* which it is, like a demon between my shoulders. To exorcise it I sometimes whistle; in English I whistle, just so, but in Gaelic *ligim fead,* I let a whistle, or *táim ag feadaíl,* I am at whistling.

I am at whistling a great deal these days, it turns out, trying to get the fear off me. For I am terrified of the fates that may befall my children—fates over which I have no power at all, not the slightest, other than keeping my little children close to me in the presence of cars and dogs and such. So there are times now, I can honestly say—for I am sometimes an honest man, and admiring always of honesty—that I am exhausted by, and frightened for, my raft of children, and in the wee hours of the night when up with one or another of the little people, I sometimes, to be honest, find myself wondering what it might have been like not to have so many.

It would have been lonely. I know this. I know it in my heart, my bones, in the chalky exhausted shiver of my soul. For there were many nights before my children came to me on magic wooden boats from seas unknown that I wished desperately for them, that I cried because they had not yet come; and now that they are here I know I pay for them every minute with fear for their safety and horror at the prospect of losing them to disease and accidents and the harsh fingers of the Lord, who taketh whomever He wishes, at which time He alone appoints, and leaves huddled and broken the father and the mother, who begged for the joy of these round faces groping for milk in the dark. So as I trudge upstairs to hold Lily in my lap, and rub my old chapped hands across the thin sharp blades of her shoulders, and shuffle with sons on shoulders in the blue hours of the night, waiting patiently for them to belch like river barges, or hear Joe happily blowing bubbles of spit in his crib simply because he can do it and is pretty proud of himself about the whole thing, or hear Liam suddenly say *ho!* for no reason other than Liamly joy at the sound of his own voice like a bell in his head, I say *yes* to them, *yes yes yes,* and to exhaustion I say *yes,* and to the puzzling wonder of my wife's love I say *O yes,* and to horror and fear and jangled joys I say *yes,* to rich cheerful chaos that leads me sooner to the grave and happier along that muddy grave road I say *yes,* to my absolute surprise and with unbidden tears I say *yes yes O yes.*

Is this a mystery and a joy beyond my wisdom?

Sea—it is.

Brian Doyle Interviews
Brian Doyle

What writers have affected and afflicted you most?

With awfulness or awe?

Either.

Jesus, make up your mind.

Both.

In English? And awful? Well, there's Jerzy Kosínski, and then there's everyone else. *Blind Date* is a book so bad I couldn't even bring myself to prop up a gimpy table with it. Wouldn't insult the table.

Anyone else?

Jerzy fills my mind to brimming at the moment. My God, the culmination of the book is a murder with an umbrella. Where was the man's editor? Talk about professional negligence. Who was responsible for marketing that book? Where are they hiding? How can they face their children? Or librarians? Or the children of librarians?

You're fixating.

I know, I know, but life's so short, and I blame Kosínski.

For the shortness of life?

Hadn't thought of that, but yes, now that I think about it, why not?

Let's change the subject. How about superb writers?

Writers or books?

Either.

Not again. Piss or get off the pot.

Okay, both, writers first.

Well, Blake, Conrad, Orwell, Twain, Stevenson, I could go on.

Go on.

I can't go on.

You must go on.

I'll go on.

Go on.

Elwyn Brooks White, Li Po, Joyce Cary, Barry Lopez, Bernard DeVoto, John Updike when he's being a literary critic, in which guise he might be the best America ever made, all due respect to Edmund Wilson, who couldn't hold Updike's jock when it comes to literary essays, and you know, while I am on the subject, I have to say that Updike's *Poorhouse Fair* was a perfect little book, and all his famous novels after that weren't as good.

Heresy.

Yeah, I know. But c'mon. The Rabbit books are Great Novels? No way. *Rabbit Run* is a very good novel and then old Rabbit gets his pecker pulled through three more. Not worth it.

You were talking superb writers.

Frank O'Connor, Patrick Kavanaugh, Wallace Stegner, Raymond Chandler, Halldór Laxness, Tolstoy, Beckett, Czesław Miłosz, Georges Simenon, Homer. Did you know there is a strain of scholarly thought that says Homer was a brilliant young woman?

No. But you were going on interminably about great writers...

Horace, Gabriel García Márquez, Jorge Amado, J. F. Powers, Seneca, Cervantes of course, Chekhov, Dostoevsky, Edward Hoagland, Tom Stoppard, Andre Dubus, John McPhee, and, my God, I nearly forgot Jorge Luis Borges, one of the greatest writers in history. Not to mention Plutarch, who might be *the* greatest writer in history.

No women?

Sweet Lord yes, dozens. Alice Munro, Mary Lavin, Flannery O'Connor, Virginia Woolf, Elizabeth Bishop, Pattiann Rogers, Muriel Spark, Margaret Atwood, who wrote one of the best essays I ever read in my life...

Which was?

"True North." Oh, God, it's terrific.

Others?

Jan Morris, Jane Austen, Marguerite Yourcenar, George Sand, Isak Dinesen, Eudora Welty, Nuala Ní Dhomhnaill, Nadine Gordimer, Annie Dillard, now we are getting into books, because Annie Dillard is a tremendous essayist but better known and justifiably so I guess as a maker of books. And there are many men like that too, Ken Kesey and Walker Percy spring to mind, who wrote well short, as essayists, but their hats rest on their books. People are always ragging on Kesey for writing crap at the end, and it is crap, but my God, the man wrote two classics, and Percy, who wrote some meandering crap too, wrote *The Moviegoer,* a classic, and a couple of perfect lesser books, like *Love in the Ruins* and *The Thanatos Syndrome.* And who am I to criticize?

Good question. Who are you to criticize?

I'm a small man who writes small essays about small matters.

So who made you god of literary criticism?

Well, first of all, you're the one who drove all the way out here to interview me, the good sweet Lord alone knows why, and second of all, you could say that criticism isn't fair unless you're John Updike or someone, that only another fine writer can accurately judge if a book is good or bad.

Would you say that?

Nah. It's bullshit.

What would you say?

That readers are very good judges of books read, for the most part. You recall what Samuel Johnson says in his *Life of Gray.*

Ah, no, not right off the top of my head.

"I rejoice to concur with the common reader; for by the common sense of readers, uncorrupted by literary prejudices, after all the refinements of subtilty and the dogmatism of learning, must be generally decided all claim to poetical honours."

That's well said.

Johnson was an eloquent bastard, by all accounts, when he wasn't swilling tea and lurching around London in one of his fits. Or guzzling port at such an alarming rate that Portugal was thinking of taking over the world for a while.

But what did he mean?

That every reader is a judge, and then the years of readers add up after a while, and the Hilaire Bellocs of the world fade and the Stevensons rise, and there, after a while, and with some discounting for fashion, you have a canon of writers who did things of grace and substance.

Are you one of those writers?

Nah. But writers are the worst judges of their work, in some ways.

High hopes?

Wicked high. There's a peculiar hope, or expectation, in writers that they will be able occasionally to make a piece of writing that is shapely, clear, direct, vigorous, witty, substantive, piercing, penetrating, astonishing, pointed, no fat, no posturing, no indulgence, something that matters greatly to the reader, something that pushes the world forward slightly, rather than just being the usual jesting in place and dancing aimlessly for the sake of entertainment in the shapeless void.

Does this happen much?

Nah. Even the best writers slump, stumble, stutter. Consistency itself isn't hard—hell, look at Jerzy Kosínski, he was consistent, all right. But consistent quality? Not even Twain or Stevenson could pull that off. Not even Shakespeare or Homer. Maybe that's why we're so dazzled by the writer who makes one perfect book and then never another word, like Harper Lee. She sure was consistent—every novel she ever made was a masterpiece, and that one novel will be in print forever. Lately I have been thinking this about Frank McCourt. *Angela's Ashes* is near perfect, and *'Tis* isn't, and whatever else he writes won't be *Angela's Ashes*. Although, Jesus, what if Stevenson had stopped after *Treasure Island,* and never wrote his essays, or *Kidnapped?* God, what a loss. Great book. Which brings to mind poor Stevenson's *Weir of Hermiston,* half-finished, the poor bastard died in the middle of it.

Speaking of books...

Oh, yes, great books. Well, the King James Bible, of course. You know the poor man who translated the Bible from its original Greek and Hebrew was executed for his pains? God forbid the Bible should get into the hands of the dirty-necked man in the street. William Tyndale. Guy was a saint.

That's it?

Nah. *Moby-Dick. Ulysses.* Cary's *The Horse's Mouth.* Marguerite Yourcenar's *Memoirs of Hadrian.* But, see, even Joyce, a hell of a great writer, wrote some crap. Did you ever read *Chamber Music?* The ravings of a sophomore. Or *Exiles?* Tinny stuff, third-rate summer stock. And *Finnegans Wake?* Listen, I read *Finnegans Wake* at the rate of one page a day for more than a year and when I got to the end I was impressed with the effort, which was herculean and admirable, but the book itself, as narrative of substance and verve? Awful. Which reminds me of Marcel Proust, the sickly bastard, and *Remembrance of Things Past,* another book I waited all my life to read. Read it. Awful. And speaking of awful, that damned James Fenimore Cooper was awful. Although, come to think of it, Twain wrote a terrific essay about how awful Cooper was, so Cooper was good for something.

You sure have a lot of spleen and bile for an essayist.

Well, I hope to work up to the spleen and bile of a novelist. Really, though, I just get annoyed at bullshit books.

Proust is bullshit?

Yeah. Face the facts. Ever read *Remembrance of Things Past?*

Yes, I did, and I found it a monumental accomplishment...

Interesting?

Pardon?

Was it interesting?

Well, it taught me a great deal about French society, and...

...it grabbed you in the gut and made your heart race and changed your life and woke you up in the night and made you cry?

It's one of the great literary accomplishments of Western civil...

It's neurasthenic bullshit, and Zane Grey was a better writer.

Well. Any other writers you think, uh, overrated?

I'm stuck on Proust at the moment. To think of all the hours wasted on his interminable salon comedy, my God. To all those readers who think Proust is the greatest thing since sliced bread, I say go read a real writer. Read the first 100 pages of *War and Peace. That's* how far you can take salon comedy and make it work. Not seven volumes of twitches and repressed longing, for Christ's sake. Get back under the covers, you wheezing pervert.

The dusk draws nigh and we had better conclude this interview. One last question: How would you rate Brian Doyle as a writer?

By trade, essayist. Commits occasional poem. As essayist, usually mumbling about love, books, hawks, or children, sometimes all four at once. Has made, I'd say, a handful of really fine essays; maybe ten, if we stretch a little. Addicted to fragmented and cascading sentences, lists, semicolons, and bang endings. Windy bastard. Best when forced into a small space. As his editor, I keep a sharp eye out for his tendency toward sentimentality, schmaltz, the scraping of badly tuned violins. His collection of essays with his dad reveals the father to be a clear, concise writer with a son happy to be a Strunk and White *Elements of Style* nightmare. Subsequent work by the son reveals a writer of occasional power and zest not at all afraid of pursuing his own peculiar obsessions and asking you to pay ten bucks for the privilege of chasing after them with him...Maybe there is a single great work in him, but I don't think so.* I think he is going to keep trying to make small perfect pieces of prose that get smaller and smaller until he finally stops writing altogether and ends his days pondering a single word, or a single letter of the alphabet, poor bastard. I'll visit him in the nuthouse.

---

* This chat between Brian and Brian was conducted in the online journal *Smokebox* and took place in 2002, when BD had published almost nothing but essays. How fascinating to find him here doubting himself even as he was mastering, among other forms: the novel; very short memoir; even shorter experimental nonfictions; his unique geometric prose form, the proem; and form-defying incantations and meditations about birds, kids, wild creatures of all colors, kinds, and sizes, his own and the larger human family, courage under extreme duress, being "rammed by joy," the glory of the Now, sneak attacks of wonder, and stories he would somehow siphon out of introverted or humble or reticent people whose stories would otherwise have remained untold.

Pants: A Note[*]

Speaking of pants, we all have favorite pants, and have had favorite pants, and in most cases, I would guess, we have worn those favorite pants down to the nubs, to the point where people who love us first made jokes and then exasperated remarks and finally shrieked when we wore those pants, and someone should call a halt in the daily ramble to celebrate the overall concept of favorite pants, and I am just that man, for I have worn several pants down to the nubs, to the point where they were first repaired here and there when fenestration occurred, and then deftly patched by the tailor, and then despaired of by the tailor, at which point they lost their legs and became shorts, but even shorts wear out eventually, and are torn asunder to finish as the household rags with which we buff our ancient automobiles, and rub mink oil into new shoes, and soak with vinegar when the windows need to be cleaned, which they do, and I had better be about the task with the last tatters of those excellent gray house-pants I loved so for the last ten years, though I was quite alone in that affection, and suffered tart and abusive remarks about them from my children, who were mortified by them, partly because I bought them for less than two dollars, and because they were shapeless, and because they had so many patches, and because I wore them with pleasure, though no other dad would be caught dead wearing pants like that, and instead of a button fastening them at the waist they had a safety pin, and be-

---

[*] The editor feels duty-bound to warn those leery of kayaking through whitewater prose without a paddle that the first paragraph of "Pants" consists, by Brian's own proud count, of a single 379-word sentence.

cause on the left side there was no pocket but only the shadow of a pocket, the pocket having declared independence from the empire of the pants at some date far in the past, an occasion I did not mourn or even really notice, until I heard the shrill plaints of my children, mortified that their dad would publicly appear in pants that were missing a pocket, and were held up by a safety pin, and were the color of nothing natural on this planet, and had been stitched and patched to the point where there were more patches than original pants.

Before those pants there were the white painters' pants I wore until they vanished one day and everyone in the house looked guilty and I never did find out what happened; and before that the white cotton coveralls I wore until the day I washed them in Boston and they actually no kidding dissolved in the washing machine, leaving a sort of bedraggled sad grainy dust I had to shovel out with a trowel; and before that I admit to a pair of bellbottom jeans, which all of us of a certain age wore at one time, though we do not admit to this willingly, and deny it when we are called on it, and lie as instantly and adamantly as we lie when asked if we ever wore desert boots, or jackets with fringes, or necklaces made with puka shells, all of which we did wear, long ago when we were young and pants had just been invented.

It is a good thing pants were invented, because without pants we could not have favorite pants, and we should, I think, occasionally pause in the river of time, and set our feet against the prevailing current, and say clearly and firmly that pants are an excellent invention, because consider the alternative, and also it should be said that slipping into your favorite pants is a subtle pleasure in the evening as you arrive home from the commercial struggle and unbuckle your corporate uniform, or on the weekend, when your pressing task for the morning is delivering a sermon on virtue to the dog.

20 Things the Dog Ate

1. Ancient Squashed Dried Round of Flat Shard of Beaver

Sweet mother of the mewling baby Jesus! You wouldn't think a creature that likes to watch Peter O'Toole movies would be such an omnivorous gobbling machine, but he has eaten everything from wasps to the back half of a raccoon. And let us not ignore the beaver. Speculation is that beaver was washed up onto road when overflowing lake blew its dam, was squashed by a truck, got flattened ten thousand times more, then summer dried it out hard and flat as a manhole cover, and the dog somehow pried it up, leaving only beaver oil on the road, and ate it. Sure, he barfed later. Wouldn't you?

2. Young Sparrow

I kid you not. Sparrow falls from nest in the pine by the fence, flutters down ungainly to unmerciful earth, dog leaps off porch like large hairy mutant arrow, gawps bird in half an instant. Man on porch roars *drop it!* Dog emits bird with a choking coughing sound as if disgusted by a misplaced apostrophe. Bird staggers for a moment and then flutters awkwardly up to fence post. I wouldn't have believed this if I had not seen it with my own holy eyeballs. Wonder how fledgling bird explained *that* adventure to mom.

3. Crayons

I don't even want to think about this ever again. Crayola. The big box—sixty-four crayons, all colors. Sure, he barfed later. Sure he did. Wouldn't you?

4. Yellow Jacket Wasps

Every summer. Even though he gets stung again and again in the nether reaches of his mouth and throat and jumps up whirling around in such a manner that we laugh so hard we have to pee. He cannot resist snapping them out of the air as if they were bright bits of candy, then making high plaintive sounds like a country singer on laughing gas. I have to pee.

5. Jellyfish on the Shore of the Vast and Impacific Pacific

Why would you ever do such a thing? What could possibly look less appetizing than an oozing quivering deceased jellyfish? Yet he does. Sure, he barfs.

6. to 19. Some Nonorganic Highlights

Pencil nubs. Lacrosse balls. The cricket ball a friend sent me from Australia. Pennies. Postcards. Sports sections. Bathrobe belts. Kindling sticks. Kazoos. Most of a paperback copy of *Harry Potter and the Order of the Phoenix*. Most of a cell-phone charger. Pen caps. Toothbrushes. One of two tiny sneakers that belonged to a child one month old, although to be fair it wasn't like the kid was actually using the sneakers.

20. An Entire Red Squirrel, Called a Chickaree in These Parts

I think the squirrel was suicidal. If you were a squirrel the size of a banana, and you could evade a dog with the athletic gifts and predatory instinct of Michael Jordan, would you venture down to the grass for any reason whatsoever, knowing that the dog could change you from present to past tense in less than a second? Would you? Me neither. But the squirrel did. The skull appeared magically in the grass two days later. The dog declined to eat the skull a second time, probably for religious reasons, or maybe because he knew he would barf. Wouldn't you?

The *Daoine Sídhe*

When our daughter, Lily, was little I left notes for her from the *daoine sídhe*, the small people, the people of peace, the hidden people, the people of the thickets. I left those notes every-where on the path up to our house, on exposed rocks, gummed to the trunks of trees with sap, slipped into the clefts of bark, folded into the quadrants of the fence. The *daoine sídhe* are not easily seen but they are there in the bushes, in the mounds and hillocks of fields, flitting among the trees, smiling in the web and braid of branches. The notes were written on the shells and hulls of nuts and the flanks of leaves and the smooth bark of white walnut twigs. The *daoine sídhe* acknowledge that the world does not be-lieve they are alive and well and adamant and elusive and interested in the doings of all beings of every sort and shape. I would try to leave a note every other day at least, and whenever I had to travel and miss a day or two of notes I felt a sag in my heart at the thought of our small Lily searching the porch and the fence and the walnut tree for notes and finding no notes and thinking perhaps the *daoine sídhe* were no longer her close and particular friends. There are many theories as to who the *daoine sídhe* are and one theory is that once they knew larger stronger crueler peo-ple were inarguably taking from them the places they loved they retreated to the shadows and the hidden places, under the ground and into the thickets, into all the half-seen half-noticed places all around us no matter where we live. We see so little. I would scrawl the notes with my left hand so that my handwriting could not be recognized and I was careful never to use a pen that she knew to be her father's pen. I learned not to leave notes from the *daoine sídhe* exposed to the rain because then the message would be washed away leaving nothing but hints and intimations. Sometimes I would leave a message without words. Another theory of the *daoine sídhe* is that they are supernatural beings but I do not think this is so. I think they are as natural and organic and present as you and me. I think that mostly what people think is supernatural isn't. I think there is much more going on than we are aware of and sensitive to and perceptive about, and the more we think we know what is possible and impossible the more we are foolish and arrogant and imprisoning ourselves in an idea. I think language is an attempt to drape words on things we sense but do not understand, like grace and the *daoine sídhe*. It is easy to say that the small people, the people of peace, the hidden people, do not exist, but you do not know that is so and neither do I, and Lily used to write back to the *daoine sídhe* on the shells and hulls of nuts and the flanks of leaves and the nubs of cedar cones and on chips of bark, and I kept every such note she ever wrote.

There came a time when I stopped writing the notes, because that time comes, and Lily stopped writing back, because that time comes, but there was a time when the *daoine sídhe* wrote to her, and she would rise from her bed, and run outside, and search the porch and the fence and the walnut tree for notes, and until the day I die I will remember the headlong eager way she ran, thrilled and anticipatory and delighted, with a warm secret in her face, because the people of peace were her friends, and wrote her name on the skins of this world, and left her little gifts and presents, and asked her questions about her people and her dreams, and the bushes and hedges and thickets and branches for her were alive with mystery and affection. And to those who would say I misled our daughter, I filled her head with airy nonsense, I soaked her in useless legend and fable and myth, I lied to her about what is present and absent in the world, I would answer, And how do you know what is possible and impossible in this world of wonders beyond our ken? Are you really so sure there is not far more than you can see, living in the half-seen half-noticed places all around us? And how is it a bad thing to fill a child's heart with joy for any reason whatsoever, on any excuse whatsoever, for as long as howsoever possible, before the world builds fences and walls around her thrilled and fervid imagination, how is that a bad thing at all?

Angeline

In the last few years before my lovely bride's aged mother died, she lived in a small apartment in a castle for elderly people in gently failing health, and I would visit her there almost every Saturday afternoon, not from a sense of duty but because I liked her wit and erudition and masterly passive aggression, which was so layered and subtle that I found myself enjoying it immensely as a form of verbal art. There are a lot of ways to be an artist and one way is to be brilliant at saying things that don't mean what you said.

I would knock on her door, even if it was slightly ajar, as it usually was, for she loved to be aware of the passing parade, and she would weakly bid me to enter, and I would shuffle in and announce cheerfully that I could stay only a few minutes, which was my opening salvo, and then we would begin a sort of conversational chess game, during which I would ask after her health, and she would say she felt well, and I would say that means everything hurts, and she would say well not *everything,* and then we would happily discuss her lengthy litany of ills and aches, and compare notes on what parts of our ships were breaking down in the most shocking and offensive manner, such that if you had bought them at a store you would be entitled to triple your money back given the egregious rate of decomposition and shoddy workmanship.

As soon as she said the word *workmanship* I would pounce, and accuse her of insulting the Force that started the universe into being, and she would pretend to be shocked at my insinuation, and then she would ask me innocently about my Mass attendance, and I would ask her innocently about the various boyfriends she had before she met her beloved late husband, and how many times exactly had she kissed each one and where the nefarious deed was done, and she would giggle in the helpless infectious way a four-year-old giggles, and we would switch to literature, but not before she made the ritual offer to get up and make me tea, which I ritually declined, but knew to be a signal for me to get up and get her a cookie from the blue cookie jar, which I really ought *not* to have, she would say, because I am so fat, and I have decided that today is the day I will go for a long walk, definitely this will happen today, perhaps right after you leave so soon, you must be so very busy to have to rush off like this each time, I am so impressed at how you manage to find time to visit a poor old lady, how very kind of you.

She never went for that walk, of course; and it took me a few visits to realize that she did not really want me to stay longer, for that would reduce and dilute the pleasurable pitch of our brief amused play for two actors; so we talked books for a few minutes (and here she had me, for she was the sort of reader who had read all of Trollope and remembered it too, which is a remarkable sort of reader, but she had a weakness for lesser poetry, which I exploited if I felt she had me on the ropes, she would be questioning me closely about Edward Gibbon and I would innocently mention Ella Wheeler Wilcox or Alfred Marmaduke Hobby and ask why her beloved 19th-century poets had to have three names, what was the deal there? and she would giggle that great giggle again), and then it was time for me to go.

I would rise and she would not, for she was old and she lived in that soft throne of a reading chair, and I would reach down and cup her face for an instant, as a form of hug or kiss, and then I would go, and we would banter as I went, for banter was our language, a way to say things without saying them; and this Saturday morning, like many other Saturday mornings since she died, I miss that. As I got to the door I would ask if she wanted another cookie and she would say *I am so fat!* and every once in a while now I really want to hear her voice in the next room, saying just exactly that.

The Way We Do Not Say What We
Mean When We Say What We Say

Of late I have been ever more absorbed by the way we do not say what we mean when we say what we say; we use all sorts of codes and keys, hints and intimations, signs and signals, to such a degree that even the most blunt and terse remarks, such as *yes* and *no*, quite often do not at all mean affirmation or negation, but rather suggest routes of negotiation, or carry loaded messages having to do with past events and discussions, or are comments on matters of a wholly different import than the one at hand; so that, for example, a quiet *no* means one thing and a loud one another, and a muttered *yes* one thing and a whispered one another, and so on in that vein; and this is not even to enter into conversation about body language, and facial expression, and eyebrow elevation, and percentage of pique, and amount of amusement, or the way that some men, and it seems to be mostly men who do this, pretend to be hard of hearing when they hear something they do not want to hear or respond to or be lured into; so that pretending to be hard of hearing turns out to sometimes be a way of saying something without having to use words, which are so often misconstrued, misapprehended, misused, or miserable altogether.

We say *yes* when we mean *I would rather not*. We say *no* when we mean *I would say yes except for all the times yes has proven to be a terrible idea*. We say *no thank you* when every fiber in our bodies is moaning *o yes please*. We say *you cannot* when what we mean is actually *you can but you sure by God ought not to*. We say *no* by staring directly at the questioner and not saying anything whatsoever. We ask questions that way also.

I am fascinated by how language is a verb and not a noun. I am riveted by how language is a process and not a preserve. I am absorbed by the way that we all speak one language but use different tones and shades and volumes and timbres and pronunciations and emphases in order to bend the language in as many ways as there are speakers of the language. Perhaps every one of us speaks a slightly different language even as we seem to be using the same words to one another. Perhaps all languages are like this although I know only this one, and this one not so well even after swimming and thrashing and singing in it since I was two and three, and learning to make sounds that turned people around in the kitchen and made them laugh or occasioned sandwiches and kisses or sent me to my room ever since I was four and five, and learning to pick out letters and gather them in gaggles and march them in parades and enjoy them spilling down pages and into my fervent dreams.

Perhaps languages use us in ways that we are not especially aware of; perhaps languages are aware that they need us to speak them, or else they go flailing into the dark to be forgotten except by stones and the oldest of trees. Perhaps languages invent themselves and then have to hunt for speakers. Perhaps all languages began from the music of insects and animals and wind through vegetative creatures. Perhaps languages began with the sound of creeks and rivers and crash of surf and whisper of tides, so that even now, eons later, when we open our mouths to speak, out comes not so much meaning and sense and reason and clarity but something of the wild world beyond understanding. Perhaps much of the reason we so often do not say what we mean to say is because we cannot; there is wild in us yet, and in every word and sentence and speech the seethe of the sea whence we came, unto which we will return, which cannot be trammeled or corralled or parsed, no matter how hard we try to mean just what we say.

On Not "Beating" Cancer

Finally, this morning, enough—one too many journalistic references to someone's "beating" cancer, as if cancer was an opponent to be defeated, an enemy to be conquered, a battle in which courage often wins the day.

It's a lie. Cancer is to be endured, that's all. The best you can hope for is to fend it off, like a savage dog, but cancer isn't defeated, it only retreats, is held at bay, retires, bides its time, changes form, regroups.

It may well be that the boy who survives an early cancer lives a long and lovely life, without ever enduring that species of illness again, but the snarl of it never leaves his heart, and you'll never hear that boy say he defeated the dark force in his bones.

Use real words. Real words matter. False words are lies. Lies sooner or later are crimes against the body or the soul. I know men, women, and children who have cancer, had cancer, died from cancer, lived after their cancer retreated, and not one of them ever used military or sporting metaphors that I remember.

All of them spoke of endurance, survival, the mad insistence of hope, the irrepressibility of grace, the love and affection and laughter and holy hands of their families and friends and churches and clans and tribes. All of them were utterly lacking in any sort of cockiness or arrogance. All of them developed a worn, ashen look born of pain and patience. And all of them spoke not of winning but of waiting.

There is a great and awful lesson there, something that speaks powerfully of human character and possibility. For all that we speak, as a culture and a people, of victory and defeat, of good and evil, of hero and coward, it is none of it quite true. The truth is that the greatest victory is to endure with grace and humor, to stay in the game, to achieve humility.

I know a boy with brain cancer. He's 16 years old. He isn't battling his cancer. It's not something to defeat. He is enduring it with the most energy and creativity and patience he can muster. He says the first year he had cancer was awful because of the fear and vomiting and surgery and radiation and chemotherapy and utter exhaustion. But he says that first year was also wonderful, because he learned to savor every moment of his days, and because he met amazing people he would never have met, and because his family and friends rallied behind him with ferocious relentless humor, and because he learned that he was a deeper and stronger and more inventive and more patient soul than he had ever imagined.

He also learned about fear, he says, because he was terrified and remains so, but he learned that he can sometimes channel his fear and turn it into the energy he needs to raise money for cancer research. Since he was diagnosed with cancer he has helped raise nearly $100,000, which is a remarkable sentence.

I met a tiny frail nun once, in Australia, while walking along a harbor, and we got to talking, and she said no one defeats cancer, cancer is a dance partner you don't want and don't like, but you have to dance, and either you die or the cancer fades back into the darkness at the other end of the ballroom.

I never forgot what she said, and think she is right, and the words we use about cancers and wars matter more than we know.

Maybe if we celebrate grace under duress rather than the illusion of total victory we will be less surprised and more prepared when illness and evil lurch into our lives, as they always will; and maybe we will be a braver and better people if we know we cannot obliterate such things, but only wield oceans of humor and patience and creativity against them. We have an untold supply of those extraordinary weapons, don't you think?

The Hawk

Recently a man took up residence on my town's football field, sleeping in a small tent in the northwestern corner, near the copse of cedars. He had been a terrific football player some years ago for our high school, and then had played in college, and then a couple of years in the nether reaches of the professional ranks, where a man might get paid a hundred bucks a game plus bonuses for touchdowns and sacks. Then he had entered into several business ventures, but these had not gone so well, and he had married and had children, but that had not gone so well either, and finally he'd taken up residence on the football field, because, he said, that was where things had gone well, and he sort of needed to get balanced again, and there was something about the field that was working for him, as far as he could tell. So, with all due respect to people who thought he was a nutcase, he decided he would stay there until someone made him leave. He had already spoken with the cops, and it was a mark of the general decency of our town that he was told he could stay as long as he didn't interfere with use of the field, which of course he would never think of doing, and it was summer, anyway, so the field wasn't in use much.

He had been nicknamed the Hawk when he was a player, for his habit of lurking around almost lazily on defense and then making a stunning strike, and he still speaks the way he played, quietly but then amazingly. When we sat on the visiting team's bench the other day, he said some quietly amazing things, which I think you should hear:

The reporter from the paper came by, he said. She wanted to write a story about the failure of the American dream and the collapse of the social contract, and she was just melting to use football as a metaphor for something or other, and I know she was just trying to do her job, but I kept telling her things that didn't fit what she wanted, like that people come by and leave me cookies and sandwiches, and the kids who play lacrosse at night set up a screen so my tent won't get peppered by stray shots, and the cops drift by at night to make sure no one's giving me grief. Everyone gets nailed at some point, so we understand someone getting nailed and trying to get back up on his feet again. I am not a drunk, and there's no politicians to blame. I just lost my balance. People are good to me. You try to get lined up again. I keep the field clean. Mostly it's discarded water bottles. Lost cellphones I hang in a plastic bag by the gate. I walk the perimeter a lot. I saw some coyote pups the other day. I don't have anything smart to say. I don't know what things mean. Things just are what they are. I never sat on the visitors' bench before, did you? Someone leaves coffee for me every morning by the gate. The other day a lady came by with twin infants, and she let me hold one while we talked about football. That baby weighed about half of nothing. You couldn't believe a human being could be so tiny—and there were two of him. That reporter, she kept asking me what I had learned, what I would say to her readers if there was only one thing I could say, and I told her, What could possibly be better than standing on a football field, holding a brand-new human being the size of a coffee cup? You know what I mean? Everything else is sort of a footnote.

The Praying Mantis Moment

A high school kid asks me this morning, *What's the greatest sports moment you ever saw?* Before my brain can rumble into gear and produce the 1986 Boston Celtics (the best basketball team I ever saw), or the 2004 Boston Red Sox (the greatest comeback in the history of baseball), or the 1969 New York Mets (for sheer shocking unbelievability, not to mention that I got to watch that whole World Series on a television in our grade school classroom—how cool was *that*), or the 1980 Miracle on Ice USA Olympic hockey team, or Doug Flutie's preposterous last-second touchdown pass for Boston College against Miami, or autistic teenager Jason McElwain drilling seven long shots in four minutes when his Athena High coach put the diligent cheerful team manager into uniform for the first time at the very end of the last home game of his senior season and he went bonkers and the whole student body went bonkers and they carried him off the floor and every time I see the film again I am elevated to tears. . . . Before I can recall any of this, I say this instead:

One time when my twin sons were little, maybe six years old, and they were playing soccer, in the town league in which every single kid I think proudly donned his or her blue uniform with blue socks every Saturday so that anywhere and everywhere you went in our town on Saturdays you would be surrounded by small blue grinning chirping people, not just on the fields and in parking lots but in burger joints and pizza places and the farmers market and the library and the grocery store, and it was a crisp beautiful golden October afternoon, and I was standing with the other parents along the sideline, half paying

105

attention and half keeping an eye out for hawks, suddenly the tiny intent players on the field all formed a loose circle on the field, and play stopped.

I remember seeing the ball roll slowly by itself into a corner of the field. I remember that the coach, one of those dads who was really into victory even though the boys and girls were three feet tall and could hardly tie their laces, was yelping and expostulating. I remember that two of the moms ran out onto the field, worried that a child was hurt. I remember that the referee, a lean long teenager who had been the most desultory and unengaged of referees up to that point, sprinted toward the circle, worried that a child was hurt.

And then the circle devolved into a sort of procession, with all the players on both teams following a girl in front, and cupped in this girl's hands was a praying mantis, which she and all the other players on both teams were escorting reverently off the field, because, as a child helpfully explained to me afterward, the praying mantis was on the field first, and maybe even lived there, while we were all visitors, and you're supposed to be polite when you visit someone's house.

I have seen many extraordinary moments in sports—stunning achievements, stunning reversals, terrific teams, teams that, at the exact moment when their absolute best and most meshed play mattered most, played even better than they ever imagined they could. But I don't think I ever saw a more *genuine* moment than the praying mantis moment. All of it was there for us to see—teamwork, decisive collective action, a leader rising to the occasion, humor, generosity, respect, surprise, narrative, drama, tension, release, grace, satisfaction, laughter, and the subtle virtue of being something you see only once in a lifetime.

IV.

This Blistering Perfect
Terrible World

Heartchitecture

Let us contemplate, you and I, the bloody electric muscle. Let us consider it from every angle. Let us remove it from its bony cage, its gristly case, and hold it to the merciless light, and turn it glinting this way and that, and look at it as if we have never seen it before, because we never *have* seen it before, not like this. Let us think carefully about the throb of its relentless tissue. Let us ponder it as the wet engine from which comes all the music we know. Let us contemplate the thousand ways it fails and the few ways it does not fail. Let us gawk at the brooding genius of its architecture. Let us consider it as the most crucial and amazing house, with its four rooms and meticulous plumbing and protein walls and chambered music. Let us dream of blood and pulse and ebb and flow. Let us consider tide and beat and throb and hum. Let us unweave the web of artery and vein, the fluttering jetties of the valves, the coursing of ions from cell to cell, the sodium that is your soul, the potassium that is your personality, the calcium that is your character.

Consider the astounding journey your blood embarks upon as it enters the pumping station of your heart. In a healthy heart, a heart that works as it has been designed to work over many millions of years by its creative and curious and tireless and nameless holy wild silent engineer, blood that has been plucked and shucked of its oxygen by the body straggles back into the right atrium, the capacious gleaming lobby of the heart.

This tired blood, dusty veteran of an immense and exhausting journey, shuffles forward to and through a small circular door in the wall, a door with three symmetrical flaps: the tricuspid valve.

This circular door opens into another big room, the right ventricle, but at the very instant this ventricle is filled to capacity with tired blood the entire ventricle *contracts!*, slamming in on itself, and our tired heroes are sent flying through the pulmonary valve and thence into the pulmonary artery, which immediately branches, carrying the blood to the right and left lungs, and there, in the joyous airy countries of the blood vessels of the lungs, your blood is given fresh clean joyous oxygen!, gobs and slathers of it!, o sweet and delicious air!, as much as those heroic blood cells can hoist aboard their tiny cellular ships, and now they resume their endless journey, heading into the marshlands and swamps of the lungs, the capillary beds, which open into the small streams and creeks called venules, which are tributaries of the pulmonary veins, of which there are four, the four magic pulmonary rivers carrying your necessary elixir back to the looming holy castle of the heart, which they will enter this time through the left ventricle, whose job is to disperse and assign the blood to the rest of the body, to send it on its quest and voyage and journey to the vast and mysterious wilderness that is You, and to tell that tale, of the journeys of your blood cells through the universe of You, would take a billion books, each alike, each utterly different.

But so much can go wrong. So much does go wrong. So many ways to go wrong. Aneurysm, angina, arrythmia, blockages and obstructions, ischemia and infection, pericarditis and pressure problems, strokes and syndromes, vascular and valvular failure. The ways that hearts falter and fail are endless. They clog and stutter. They sigh and stop. They skip a beat. They lose the beat. Or they beat so fast and madly that they endure electrical frenzies. One electrical frenzy is called circus movement: the electrical impulse leaves the rhythmic world of contraction-and-rest and enters a state of essentially continuous beat. A heart in circus movement may beat five hundred times a minute for as long as ninety seconds before it stops altogether and the person wrapped around that heart dies.

Consider those ninety seconds. A minute and a half. The fastest and last minute and a half of that one life. A minute and a half tipped forward into relentless irretrievable headlong final free fall. The heart sprinting toward oblivion, unable to rest, revving into chaos; achieving, for the last ninety seconds of its working life, a state of such intense beat that it comes as close to beatlessness as it ever could while beating: until it ceases to beat.

Or think of the heart as a music machine—not a far-fetched idea, for the heart runs on electric impulse and does so in a steady 4/4 rhythm. A musician friend of mine maintains that the 4/4 rhythm, standard in popular music, feels right, feels normal, because it is the pace of our hearts, the interior music we hear all day and all night. We are soaked in the song of the heart every hour of every year every life long.

Fill my heart with song, sings Frank Sinatra, and is your heart filled with pain?, sings Elvis Presley, and my heart will go on, sings Celine Dion, and open your heart, sings Elton John, and open your heart, sings Lenny Kravitz, and he had a heart of glass, sings Blondie, and I've been a miner for a heart of gold, sings Neil Young, and don't be blind heart of mine, rasps Bob Dylan, and why does my heart feel so bad, moans Moby, and put a little love in your heart, sings Annie Lennox, and everybody's got a hungry heart, roars Bruce Springsteen, and my heart still beats, sings Beyoncé, and Lord with glowing heart I'd praise Thee, sang Francis Scott Key, and stop draggin' my heart around, snarls Tom Petty, and I got them broken heart blues, moans Sonny Boy Williamson, and I canna live without the inarticulate speech of the heart, sings the genius Van Morrison, and this is the last chance for hearts of stone, sings Southside Johnny Lyon, and unchain my heart, sings Joe Cocker, and what would rock and pop and blues and gospel and jazz and soul and rap do without this most necessary musical organ? Would there even be such a thing as music if there were no hearts to break and fill and unchain and hijack?

It weighs eleven ounces. It feeds a vascular system that comprises sixty thousand miles of veins and arteries and capillaries. It beats a hundred thousand times a day. It shoves two thousand gallons of blood through the body every day. It begins when a fetus is three weeks old and a cluster of cells begins to pulse with the cadence of that particular person, a music and rhythm and pace that will endure a whole lifetime. No one knows why the cluster of cells begins to pulse at that time or with that beat. These cells undergo what is called spontaneous depolarization. Channels inside these cells begin to leak sodium and the wash of sodium sparks the trading of potassium and calcium back and forth which inspires an electrical current which, augmented, is the beat of your heart. These cells are infectious, as it were: if you put them alongside any other type of cell in the body, they make the other cells beat to their beat.

The heart is the first organ to form. It is smaller than a comma when it begins, and ends up bigger than a fist. Every cell in it is capable of pulsing. No one knows how that could be. The pulse begins when a baby is about twenty days old. No one knows why it happens then. The pulse then continues, on average, for about two billion pulses, and no one knows why that many, or that few. Why not one billion per creature? Why not twenty billion? Mayflies to mastodons, beetles to bison, prophets to poets, infants to infanticides, all are issued the same number of pulses to do with what they will. *Tell me,* asks the great quiet American poet Mary Oliver, *what is it you plan to do with your one wild and precious life?*

Consider the engineering of the heart. It begins life as a primitive hollow tube of tissue which bends and loops and twists and turns and envelops and overlaps and intricately creates itself as a heart, the wings and tendrils of tissue advancing and retreating, holes and spaces appearing, walls and valves constructing themselves according to a mysterious and extraordinary command and design, all this infinitesimal heartchitecture bathed in the one fluid in the ancient universe that can sustain the new wet machine: rich fresh blood from the mother, which she sends through the placenta to her developing child in oxygenated bursts to the new brain, the new heart, the rest of the new body.

Here are some magic numbers: all mothers at all times past and present to all children developing under their hearts send 62 percent of placental blood to the new brains, 29 percent to the new body, and 9 percent to the new heart. Hitler and Ho, Gandhi and Gautama, Mohammed and Maimonides, Mao and Moses, the Madonna and her mother, the Madonna and her Child: when they were fingers of flesh floating in their mothers, new ideas clinging to uterine walls, they received blood from their mothers in exactly the same doses.

In America these days one woman dies every minute of every day from a failed heart. More women die of failed hearts than men. Failed hearts kill more women and men than the next seven causes of death combined. The highest rate of death by failed heart is in Utah. The lowest rate is in Mississippi. More than four hundred babies are born every day with flawed hearts. One percent of all babies born all over the world are born with flawed hearts. Twenty percent of all babies born with flawed hearts will die before their first birthday.

Our body fluids contain about one percent salt, nowadays—very likely the exact salinity of whatever ancient sea we managed to crawl out of, a sea we could leave because we had learned, first of all, to contain it; and that sea is contained and remembered most crucially now in the heart, where salt sloshes back and forth between cells, forming the first thrum of the heartbeat, first hint of the absolute and necessary note from which comes the salt song of You.

The Greatest Nature Essay Ever

...would begin with an image so startling and lovely and wondrous that you would stop riffling through the rest of the mail, take your jacket off, sit down at the table, adjust your spectacles, tell the dog to lie *down*, tell the kids to make their own sandwiches for heaven's sake, that's why god gave you *hands*, and read straight through the piece, marveling that you had indeed seen or smelled or heard *exactly* that, but never quite articulated it that way, or seen or heard it articulated that way, and you think, *man, this is why I read nature essays, to be startled and moved like that, wow.*

The next two paragraphs would smoothly and gently move you into a story, seemingly a small story, a light tale, easily accessed, something personal but not self-indulgent or self-absorbed on the writer's part, just sort of a cheerful nutty everyday story maybe starring an elk or a mink or a child, but then there would suddenly be a sharp sentence where the dagger enters your heart and the essay spins on a dime like a skater, and you are plunged into waaay deeper water, you didn't see it coming at all, and you actually shiver, your whole body shimmers, and much later, maybe when you are in bed with someone you love and you are trying to evade his or her icy feet, you think, *my god, stories do have roaring power, stories are the most crucial and necessary food, how come we never hardly say that out loud?*

The next three paragraphs then walk inexorably toward a line of explosive Conclusions on the horizon like inky alps. Probably the sentences get shorter, more staccato. Terser. Blunter. Shards of sentences. But there's no opinion or commentary, just one line fitting into

114

another, each one making plain inarguable sense, a goat or even a senator could easily understand the sentences and their implications, and there's no shouting, no persuasion, no eloquent pirouetting, no pronouncements and accusations, no sermons or homilies, just calm clean clear statements one after another, fitting together like people holding hands.

Then an odd paragraph, this is a most unusual and peculiar essay, for right here where you would normally expect those alpine Conclusions, some Advice, some Stern Instructions and Directions, there's only the quiet murmur of the writer tiptoeing back to the story he or she was telling you in the second and third paragraphs. The story slips back into view gently, a little shy, holding its hat, nothing melodramatic, in fact it offers a few gnomic questions without answers, and then it gently slides away off the page and off the stage, it almost evanesces or dissolves, and it's only later after you have read the essay three times with mounting amazement that you see quite how the writer managed the stagecraft there, but that's the stuff of another essay for another time.

And finally the last paragraph. It turns out that the perfect nature essay is quite short, it's a lean taut thing, an arrow and not a cannon, and here at the end there's a flash of humor, and a hint or tone or subtext of sadness, a touch of rue, you can't quite put your finger on it but it's there, a dark thread in the fabric, and there's also a shot of espresso hope, hope against all odds and sense, but rivetingly there's no call to arms, no clarion brassy trumpet blast, no website to which you are directed, no hint that you, yes you, should be ashamed of how much water you use or the car you drive or the fact that you just turned the thermostat up to seventy, or that you actually have not voted in the past two elections despite what you told the kids and the goat. Nor is there a rimshot ending, a bang, a last twist of the dagger. Oddly, sweetly, the essay just ends with a feeling eerily like a warm hand brushed against your cheek, and you sit there, near tears, smiling, and then you stand up. Changed.

The Creature Beyond the Mountains

There are fish in the rivers of Cascadia that are bigger and heavier than the biggest bears. To haul these fish out of the Columbia River, men once used horses and oxen. These creatures are so enormous and so protected by bony armor that no one picks on them, so they grow to be more than a hundred years old, maybe two hundred years old; no one knows. Sometimes in winter they gather in immense roiling balls in the river, maybe for heat, maybe for town meetings, maybe for wild sex; no one knows. A ball of more than sixty thousand of them recently rolled up against the bottom of a dam in the Columbia, causing a nervous United States Army Corps of Engineers to send a small submarine down to check on the dam. They eat fish, clams, rocks, fishing reels, shoes, snails, beer bottles, lamprey, eggs, insects, fishing lures, cannonballs, cats, ducks, crabs, basketballs, squirrels, and many younger members of their species; essentially, they eat whatever they want. People have fished for them using whole chickens as bait, with hooks the size of your hand. They like to follow motorboats, for reasons no one knows. As with human beings, the males wish to spawn in their early teens, but the females wait until their twenties. The females then produce epic rafts of eggs, 3 or 4 million at a time, from ovaries that can weigh more than two hundred pounds. On average three of those eggs will grow to be mature fish. Some of the fish that have been caught have been fifteen feet long and weighed fifteen hundred pounds. There are stories of fish more than twenty feet long and two thousand pounds. A fish that long would be taller than three Shaquille O'Neals and heavier than six. There is a persistent legend in southwest Washington State that somewhere in the water near Mount Saint Helens is the biggest fish of this kind that anyone has ever seen or heard about or imagined, a fish so big that when it surfaces it is occasionally mistaken for a whale, but this is the same region of the wild and wondrous world where Sasquatch is thought to most likely live, so you wonder.

The being of which we speak is *Acipenser transmontanus,* the sturgeon beyond the mountains, popularly called the white sturgeon, although it is not white, but as gray as the moist lands in which it lives, the temperate rainforest west of the Pacific mountains and east of the not-very-Pacific Ocean. From northern Mexico to southern Alaska it cruises the nether reaches of rivers, battling only the sea lions that in recent years have taken up residence in the coastal rivers of the West to dine on salmon and young sturgeon, but I am sure there will come a day when I will pick up my newspaper and read about a precipitous decline in sea-lion pups, and I will remember that a new lion pup is not much bigger than a chicken or a cat or a basketball. Taking the long view, you have to admire the individual sturgeon, very probably adolescent males, who over the years were the first to eat such things as cats and cannonballs. Perhaps it was accidental, but perhaps not, perhaps it was a brave leap, and among the sturgeon of today there are legends of the first heroes who inhaled volleyballs and badgers. This could be.

At the Sturgeon Viewing and Interpretive Center at the Bonneville Fish Hatchery in Cascade Locks, Oregon, where Tanner Creek empties into the Columbia River, near the immense Bonneville Dam, there are three enormous sturgeon in a large open pond. Two of them, each about eight feet long and weighing about an eighth of a ton, have not as yet been given names by human beings. The third is Herman, the most famous sturgeon in Oregon. Herman is more than ten feet long and weighs almost five hundred pounds. No one knows how old he is. He might be ninety years old. There are references to Herman the Sturgeon in hatchery records beginning in 1925. It is thought that there have been several Hermans, some exhibited annually at the Oregon State Fair. This Herman, who is probably not the 1925 Herman, arrived at Bonneville ten years ago, a mere nine feet and four hundred pounds, then. Many thousands of people come to see Herman every year, as they visit the hatchery's spawning rooms, holding ponds, rearing ponds, and egg-incubation building, all of which are for salmon and steelhead; the three sturgeon here, and the pool of massive rainbow trout, are show ponies only, sturgeon and trout not being as close to extinction as salmon and steelhead. This hatchery alone raises a million coho salmon, 8 million chinook, and 300,000 steelhead every year, for release into various Oregon rivers. There are fish everywhere at the hatchery, leaping and milling and swirling and startling visitors, and it is remarkable and piercing to see so many miracles at once, so many mysterious beings, so many individual adventures, so much excellent flaky accompaniment to fine wine, and to think where they will go and what they will see, some of them headed into the deepest thickets of the ocean, others into the bellies of animals of every size and shape, but pretty much every human visitor is here also to see Herman, and I station myself in a dark corner of the center one afternoon and view the human beings who come to view Herman.

There are nuns. There are schoolchildren. There is a man wearing a cat on his shoulder. There is a woman wearing not much more than a smile. There is a woman wearing white plastic thigh boots and a baseball jacket. There is a deputy mayor. There is a long-haul truck driver smoking a cigar that smells like something died in his truck. There are teenagers holding hands. There is a man dressed head to toe in Seattle Seahawks fan gear, including sneakers. There is a man with a cane and a woman with a walker. There is a girl in a wheelchair. There are tour groups, family outings, and a man wearing tuxedo trousers and gleaming black shoes and a motorcycle gang jacket. People eat and drink and joke and curse and smoke and spit and gape and dawdle and laugh and several ask me, Where's Herman? I say my experience is that he will loom into view after a while. Some people don't wait. Some people express annoyance with the hatchery management and the lack of organization as regards Herman's appearance. Others mistake Herman's eight-foot-long companions for Herman. Others wait silently for Herman to loom into view.

The most memorable viewing for me that day was a young man with a small boy who appeared to be his son. The father looked like he was about nineteen, with the wispy first mustache and chin-bedraggle of a teenager. The boy, wearing a red cowboy hat, seemed to be about three years old. The father tried to line the boy up for a photograph, tried to get the kid to stand still until Herman loomed into view, but the boy skittered here and there like a rabbit, the father alternately wheedling and barking at him, and finally the boy stood still, but facing the wrong direction, with his nose pressed against the glass, and the father sighed and brought his camera down to his waist at exactly the moment that Herman slowly filled the window like a zeppelin. The boy leaped away from the window and his hat fell off. No one said a word. Herman kept sliding past for a long time. Finally, his tail exited stage left and the boy said, awed, clear as a bell, *Holy shit, Dad*. The father didn't say anything and they stood there another couple of minutes, both of them speechless, staring at where Herman used to be, and then they walked up the stairs holding hands.

On the way home to Portland, as I kept an eye out for osprey along the banks of the Columbia, I thought of that boy's face as Herman slid endlessly past the window. It's hilarious what he said, it's a great story, I'll tell it happily for years, but what lingers now for me is his utter naked amazement. He saw ancientness up close and personal. He saw a being he never dreamed was alive on this planet, a being he never imagined, a being beyond vast, a being that rendered him speechless with awe until he could articulate a raw blunt astonishment that you have to admire for its salty honesty. He saw wonder, face-to-face. Maybe wonder is the way for us with animals in the years to come. Maybe wonder is the way past the last million years of combat and into the next million years of something other than combat. Maybe the look on that kid's face is the face of the future.

The woman who married me, a slight mysterious riveting being not half as tall as Herman, grabs me by the beard in the kitchen one day and says, What is *up* with you and sturgeon? And I spend days afterward trying to answer this question for myself.

Part of it is bigness. The fact that there are wild creatures bigger and heavier than cars *right there in the river in a city of two million,* is astounding, and it is also astounding that everyone totally takes this for granted, whereas I would very much like to stop people in the street about this matter, and blast-text *OMG!!!,* and set up a continual river-bottom video feed in all grade schools so kids everywhere in my state will quietly mutter, *Holy shit, Dad,* and establish the website MassiveSturgeonVisitation.com, so when a creature the size of a kindergarten bus slides to the surface suddenly in front of a Cub Scout hunting up crawdads in the Columbia, he, the Cub Scout, can post an alert as soon as he changes his underwear. And the bigness of sturgeon here is mysteriously stitched, for me, into the character and zest and possibility of Cascadia; there are huge things here, trees and fish and mountains and rivers and personalities and energies and ideas, and somehow the pairing of power and peace in the piscatorial is a hint of the possible in people.

Part of it is harmlessness; they don't eat us, no matter how often we eat them. Adult sturgeon do not even have teeth, having dropped their weapons after gnashing through adolescence. We have a fairly straightforward relationship with most animals: we kill the ones who eat us, and we eat the rest. Most of the ones who eat us are bigger than we are—crocodiles, tigers, sharks, bears—but there are some animals that are bigger than we are that don't eat us, and at those we gape, and grope for some other emotion beyond paranoia and palate and pet. Whales, for example. We yearn for something with enormous gentle animals, something more than mammalian fellowship. We want some new friendship, some sort of intimate feeling for which we don't have good words yet.

Part of it is sheer goofy wonder; I suppose to me sturgeon are a lovely example of all the zillions of things we do not know, for all our brilliance and inventiveness and cockiness, all our seeming confidence that we run the world. Most of what we do know is that we don't know hardly anything, which cheers me up wonderfully. The world is still stuffed with astonishments beyond our wildest imagining, which is humbling, and lovely, and maybe the only way we are going to survive ourselves and let everything else alive survive us too.

Part of it is freshwaterness. The ocean is the densest wilderness on the planet, the jungle, the unexplored deep, filled with mysteries and monsters, mostly unmapped, the endless blue world where human beings are unmoored; whereas the rivers are land veins, serpentine lakes, people paths, arteries through the muscled earth; and we are more comfortable in general with fresh water, which we drink and in which we bathe, than with salt, which we cannot drink and in which we are not only uncomfortable but essentially unwelcome. Even the biggest rivers and lakes are stories with endings, they can be plumbed, they are the land's liquid cousins, the land embraces them; whereas the ocean is landless, endless wilderness, its denizens often savage and terrifying. So to ponder an enormous creature that is not terrifying, that lives in the river I can see from my office window, that remains pretty much a total mystery to biologists and ichthyologists and the United States Army Corps of Engineers—this gives me hope.

I ask fisherfolk what it's like to haul up a big sturgeon from the bottom of a river. Like dragging a refrigerator, says one man. Like fishing for bear, says another. Like having an air conditioner on the end of your line and if you give it slack it will sink and if you pull too hard you will snap your line, so basically you are doomed to an hour's weight lifting, at the end of which you haul up a nightmare from the Paleozoic, says another.

They have the most subtle bite, says a man who guides men and women to sturgeon in the mouth of the Mighty Columbia. We call it a soft bite. You're hardly aware your hook's been taken until you set and pull and realize there's a dinosaur on your line. And they're very fast. People don't think they are quick because they get so big. People think they are like manatees or whatever, but I've seen them rip off fifty yards of line in ten seconds. They dart, man. Something to see, a ten-foot animal *whipping* through the water, and they jump like tarpon, and they tail-walk especially in shallow water, and the first time you hook a serious dinosaur and he or she decides to light out for the territory you're...flabbergasted. Awed. Fascinating animal. Very, very adaptable. They live deep, they live shallow, they eat everything, their only enemies are sea lions and us. What else can I tell you? They have the worst eyesight imaginable, but they have a very sharp sense of smell. One sturgeon tagged in the Columbia showed up in San Francisco Bay. Others go out in the ocean and disappear for years. No one knows what they're doing or how far they travel. Isn't that wild? We think we know everything science-wise but the fact is we know about half of nothing.

People tell me sturgeon stories. A man frying oysters in a restaurant in Portland tells me that his grandpa told him there used to be so many sturgeon in the Columbia that you couldn't use a net because it would for sure get broke. A biologist from Texas tells me that sturgeon evolved into their current form long before there was a hint of person in the world. The journalist Richard Carey notes that there are stories of sturgeon in the Volga River in Russia weighing nine thousand pounds, which would be twenty-eight Shaquille O'Neals, and that some sturgeon species can whistle, and that the Kootenai Indians of Idaho used to harpoon sturgeon from canoes they designed to be dragged by the fish until it was exhausted and could be hauled aboard or towed to shore: sturgeon surfing. An anatomist friend of mine explains that sturgeon have cousins among the bony fishes who emerge from the water and wander around on land for brief periods looking for good things to eat, and that they have other cousins who build up speed to about forty miles an hour underwater and then leap out of the water and glide through the air for more than five hundred feet, which is seventy-one Shaquille O'Neals, and that sturgeon themselves, along with their closest cousins the paddlefish, have such extraordinarily sensitive sensory barbels—the four long whiskerlike tissues between mouth and nose that look not unlike a teenage boy's first uncertain mustache—that they may be able to discern what *kind* of cat they are about to eat. This could be.

I kept coming back to Herman. Every once in a while, I would find myself thinking about him and soon I would be in the car sailing through the stunning Columbia Gorge to stand quietly in the shadowy corner of his viewing room for a while. Without fail, every time I was there someone would be startled and say something startling. It wasn't always a kid. One time a small man with a mohawk haircut said something in a language I don't know, but his tone was unmistakable and I would bet the house he said *holy shit* in Mayan or Tagalog or whatever. Another time a man knelt and prayed when Herman hove into view. Another time a young woman came in and watched Herman for a while and then whirled on me and delivered a sudden tart lecture on how it was a *sin* and a *crime* to jail this fellow living being in this ridiculous *circus,* to which I didn't reply, there being nothing to say, and she stomped off.

I went and sat by the river for a long time after that, though. She was right; Herman is in prison for the crime of being amazing, which doesn't seem altogether fair. And for all you can say that he's safe, and well fed, and has lots of visitors to his jail cell, and cool roommates, and a certain renown, especially among children, still, he is confined without cause, and chances are excellent that he would rather be in the river, gorging on salmon and whistling at girls and eating cats and basketballs like the other guys.

I end up at the edge of the Mighty Columbia, which is thought to be maybe 10 million years old and which was brawling past this spot, crammed with *Acipenser transmontanus,* long before my forebears wandered out of Africa, gaping at the wider world. A heron lumbers over, looking like a blue tent. In front of me the Bonneville Dam stretches forever. Sturgeon live so long that there are certainly elders above the dam, upriver, who were there before the first lock was built in 1938. Perhaps they are wondering when the sudden wall in the water will dissolve. Perhaps the vast ball of sturgeon that boiled at the base of the dam in early 2008 was motivated not by lust or politics or sea-lion revenge plots but by the itch to communicate with loved ones behind the Wall.

I go back and watch Herman for a while and consider that maybe his job is to be an agent of wonder. Maybe everyone who gapes at Herman gets a sturgeon seed planted in their dreams. Maybe Herman is the one among his clan chosen to awaken the walk-uprights. Maybe he watches the people who watch him and every time a child leaps back amazed Herman silently scores another one for the good guys. Maybe he is here to grant us humility, because humility and wonder of sturgeonly shape and proportion naturally swim to wisdom.

Hoop

Photographs are time machines, and other people's children are time machines (how did that kid get a foot taller and an octave deeper in a month?), and boxes of old letters and cards are time machines, and old people's memories are the best time machines (my mom just told me about going to minor-league baseball games in New York City *80 years ago*), but often smells and sounds and glances are terrific time machines, as I can presently attest, having just seen a boy of 12 or so bicycle past with a basketball under his arm, and suddenly it is 1968 and I am that boy and I am pedaling home from the gym after my First Official Practice with a Real Team, this after a thousand hours of playing in parks and playgrounds with my brothers, and I made the team, and got a jersey (number 42, for my hero Connie Hawkins), which is so precious to me that I have it huddled under my jacket so that not a drop of rain or speck of mud shall touch and stain it, and I am the happiest boy who ever lived on this wild bright planet, and now I know that the game I love above all other games is going to be my dear and close companion this year while I wear the green and gold for Saint John Vianney, and perhaps I have the secret sense that the game and I will be the dearest of friends for the next 20 years, until my back gives up and I have to quit suddenly and never play again and never even pick up a ball again, and dream almost nightly about playing ball quick and confident and intent until I am deep into my 40s, and write about the game and its denizens every year the rest of my life, as, for example, here.

Just as the boy turns the corner of the next street he actually begins

125

to dribble the ball while still riding his bicycle, which delights me all the more because I did the same thing at his age, thinking of it as yet another cool training exercise much like taping cardboard across the bottoms of my spectacles so I could not see the ball while dribbling, and playing with ankle weights in practice so that I would soar all the more weightlessly in games, and dribbling for miles along paths and trails using only my left hand, and not coming into the house at dusk until I hit 10 straight shots from both of my preferred spots on the floor, and learning to sink hook shots by recruiting my much taller brothers to play defense which they did with burly alacrity and rough-housery, and dribbling between and around my legs for 20 minutes with each hand, not to be tricky or show off, but so that I could rely on the skill unconsciously if a sudden change of direction was called for in a tight spot during a game, and practicing every sort of bank and spin shot on the same theory, and a thousand more things, and these memories do not make me sad or nostalgic but rather thrilled and happy that I had those hours. No man ever savored those hours in the game more than I did, no man in the history of the world; and rather than sigh at their loss, I sing at their gain.

Our Daily Murder

Bless me, Father, for I have sinned, and I am totally wrestling with feeling bad about sinning, which I do a little and then don't at all—I'll explain. Yesterday a guy walked into a classroom in my state and shot nine people to death and shot up ten others so bad that they'll limp and be in pain in a dozen ways every hour the rest of their lives. A cop shot the shooter and now the shooter is dead. But this all happened too in Columbine and Aurora and Sandy Hook and Charleston and Norway and Dunblane and Tasmania and on and on and need I go on? And what is my sin? I'll tell you, Father. Lean in a little here so no one hears. I wanted to shoot the shooters. In the head. I did. And then when I calmed down I wanted to punch the idiots who immediately started shouting that this doesn't have anything to do with gun control. And then I wanted to thump the people who excoriated the school for not having armed guards on duty every fifty feet around the perimeter. And then I wanted to afflict everyone issuing comment and opinion and advice and sound bites with laryngitis that would last a month. And then all I could see were body bags and people sobbing. The mother and the father of the shooter sobbing and speechless. And I was ashamed of myself, Father, because I wriggle with violent impulses, and I have punched and thumped and shouted, and in me is the same squirm of lashing violence as in every other man and probably most women, if they were honest. So I come to you, Father, to see if you can help me. I need you to tell me this will end someday. I need you to tell me Christ was right and turning the other cheek will not always mean getting a knife slash on the other cheek too. I need you to tell me that this has nothing to do with easy useless labels like Satan and Evil and Insanity and everything to do with the brooding shadow in every heart. I need you to tell me that shadow will be dispersed and disseminated someday and not by fiat from the One but by us working our asses off to make violence something that you visit in war museums. I need you to confirm that it's us who can solve our daily murder. I need you to confirm that Christ is in us and we can do this if we stop posturing and preening and labeling and actually do something about lonely idiots with brains full of worms. And we are not just talking about addled lonely boys with squirming brains, are we? Aren't we also talking about arrogant pompous blowhards like bin Laden and Hitler who are sure they know what's best and right for everyone? Aren't we talking about slimy wannabe caliphs who want to own a desert where they pretend it's the seventh century? Aren't we talking about everyone who thinks they know best? Aren't we talking about that jagged splinter of bloody bile in every man's heart and probably most women, if they were honest? Aren't we talking about your heart and mine, Father? What's my sin, really? Deeper than the rage I feel with people who murder innocents, people who close up their brains as they open their mouths, my sin, down deep, is that I often despair of us, Father. I do. At night. I don't wake my wife. She has enough to deal with. But I lie awake and think maybe we are exactly the same savage primates we were a million years ago, and culture and civilization are mere veneer, and we will always be pulling triggers in so many ways—pistols, rifles, cannons, drones, bombers, warheads, whatever brilliant murder tool we come up with next. We're so creative, eh, Father? Always looking for a new way to blow the other guy to bits and then drape righteous excuse over the bloody dirt. So that's what I wanted to tell you, Father. I rage, I despair. I am ashamed of that. Both are small. I want to be big. I want us all to be big. I want Christ to be right. I want the word *shooter* to be forgotten. I want us to outwit violence. But I am so often so afraid that we will always be small and that Christ was a visionary whose words will drown in a tsunami of blood. I know you can't forgive me, Father. I know the drill. But I ask that you join me in intercession to the One for hope, for endurance, for a flash of his love like water when we are so desperately thirsty we think we will never find water again. Amen.

Because It's Hard

I was in a monastery the other day and got to talking to a monk who, when I asked him why he was a monk—why he volunteered for a job liable to loneliness, a commitment to an idea no one can ever prove or document, a task that entails years of labor in the belief that somehow washing dishes and cutting grass and listening to pain and chanting in chapel matters in the long scheme of things—said, because it's hard.

I was startled; sure I was. You would be, too. Rarely do people say with a grin that they do something because it's hard to do it. But he said it again, still smiling, and then he talked about it for a while, haltingly at first, as he felt for the words, and then with a lovely flow, like something let loose from a dam after a long time pooling behind the dam.

Because I am not sure I can do it at all, he said, let alone do it well, and do it for years and years, perhaps for my whole life. I cannot think that way. I try to be a good monk for a week at a time. Walking helps greatly, I find. Also birds. We have a resident heron here who has been a great help to me. Sometimes he or she is right there by the reeds when I am in pressing need of a heron. I have come to think that the birds are shards of faith themselves in mysterious ways. You could spend a whole life contemplating birds and never come to the end of the amazing things they do. There are many swallows here and I spend hours at a time watching them conduct their intricate maneuvers. They have the loveliest gentle chitter with which they speak to each other in the air. Remarkable creatures altogether. When I was first a monk I was of a mind to adopt one as a pet, and I actually got a ladder and climbed to one of their nests, but when I loomed into view there, surely a great horror to the parents and the young ones, I could not find it in myself to reach in and steal a child. I went back down the ladder and went to the chapel.

I want to be a monk because I think that would be a very good use of me, he continued. Does that sound strange? It sounds a bit arrogant, I suppose. I don't mean to be arrogant. I want to be an implement. Something like a shovel with a beard. If I live with humility and intent, if I do what I do well and gracefully, that is good. Beyond that I cannot go. When I speak to children they will ask me things like, if I do enough good, and other people do good, then the good stacks up, right? and the good eventually beats the bad, right? and I cannot say this is so. I am not very interested in speculation about such things. I was never interested in theology. I think theology is an attempt to make sense of that to which sense does not apply. I cannot explain why I hope that what I do matters; all I can do is do what I do, either well or ill, patiently or not, gracefully or not. And I do find that doing things mindfully, patiently, easefully, makes the task far more interesting. I love to cut the grass here, for I sometimes come to a sort of understanding with the grass, and the hill, and the creatures in the grass, and with my legs and arms and back, a sort of silent conversation in which we all communicate easily and thoroughly. Do you have any idea of what I mean with all this?

I think I do, I said. I have children and a fascinating graceful mysterious wife and sometimes we are like five fingers in a hand. And sometimes when I write, that happens, that the page and my fingers and my dreams are all the same thing for an hour. I always emerge startled.

Yes, he said, yes, *that* is why I am a monk. I thought perhaps I could add to that larger music, by being a monk. I might have held almost any job, I suppose, been any sort of man—I was very lucky in life, and had a wonderful childhood, and education, and I loved women, and they loved me, and I might have been happy and fulfilled in a dozen ways. But I knew inside that I had to try to do what was hard for me to do, to be of best use.

That's well said, I said.

Then perhaps I was a good monk during the saying of it, he said, smiling again. And now I must be off. Perhaps my best use for the last few minutes was to talk to you; and now my work is certainly to clean the kitchen, for it is Wednesday, and it is my job to make the kitchen shine. Come down a little early tomorrow, before everyone else is up, and see if I have been a good monk for the next couple of hours. Sleep well. The birds begin to sing at about four in the morning. It is my belief that the warblers are first but I could be wrong. A better monk would know, but I am not yet a good monk in that area, though I have hopes.

Irreconcilable Dissonance

I have been married once, to the woman to whom I am still married so far, and one thing I have noticed about being married is that it makes you a lot more attentive to divorce, which used to seem like something that happened to other people, but doesn't anymore, because of course every marriage is pregnant with divorce, and also now I know a lot of people who are divorced, or are about to be, or are somewhere in between those poles, for which shadowy status there should be words like *mivorced* or *darried* or *sleeperated* or *schleperated,* but there aren't, so far.

People seem to get divorced for all sorts of reasons, and I find myself taking notes, probably defensively, but also out of sheer amazement at the chaotic wilderness of human nature. For example, I read recently about one man who got divorced so he could watch all sixty episodes of *The Wire* in chronological order. Another man got divorced after thirty years so he could, he said, fart in peace. Another man got divorced in part because he told his wife he had an affair, but he didn't have an affair, he just couldn't think of any other good excuse to get divorced, and he didn't want to have an affair, or be with anyone else other than his wife, because he liked his wife, and rather enjoyed her company as a rule, he said, but he just didn't want to be married to her every day anymore, he preferred to be married to her every second or third day, but she did not find that a workable arrangement, and so they parted company, confused.

Another man I read about didn't want to get divorced, he said, but when his wife kept insisting that they get divorced because she had

133

fallen in love with another guy, he, the husband, finally agreed to get divorced, and soon after he found himself dating the other guy's first wife; as the first guy said, who could invent such a story?

I read about a woman who divorced her husband because he picked his nose. I read about a woman who got divorced because her husband never remembered to pay their property taxes and finally, she said, it was just too much. Is it so very much to ask, she asked, that the person who shares responsibility for your life remembers to pay your joint taxes? Does this have to be a crisis every year? She seemed sort of embarrassed to say what she said, but she said it.

It seems to me that the reasons people divorce are hardly ever for the dramatic reasons that we assume are the reasons people get divorced, like snorting cocaine for breakfast or discovering that the minister named Bernard who you married ten years ago is actually a former convict named Ezzard with a wife in Wisconsin, according to the young detective who sat down in your office at the accounting firm one morning and sounded embarrassed about some things he had come to tell you that you should know.

I read about a couple who got divorced because of *irresolute differences,* a phrase that addled me for weeks. Another couple filed for divorce on the grounds of *irreconcilable dissonance,* which seemed like one of those few times in life when the exact right words are applied to the exact right reason for those words. I read about another woman who divorced her husband because one time they were walking down the street, the husband on the curb side in accordance with the ancient courteous male custom of being on that side so as to receive the splatter of mud or worse from the street and keep such splatter from the pristine acreage of his beloved, and as they approached a fire hydrant he lifted his leg, puppylike, as a joke, and she marched right to their lawyer's office and instituted divorce proceedings. That particular woman refused to speak to reporters about the reasons for divorce, but you wonder what the iceberg was under that surface, you know?

The first divorce I saw up close, like the first car crash you see up close, is imprinted on the inside of my eyelids, and I still think about it, not because it happened, but because years after it happened it seems so fated to have happened. How could it be that two people who really liked each other, and who took a brave crazy leap on not just living together, which lots of mammals do, but swearing fealty and respect in front of a huge crowd, and filing taxes as a joint entity, and spawning a child, and cosigning mortgages and car loans, how could they end up signing settlement papers on the dining-room table and then wandering out into the muddy garden to cry? How could that be?

The saddest word I've heard wrapped around divorce like a tattered blanket is *tired,* as in "We were both just tired," because being tired seems so utterly normal to me, so much the rug always bunching in that one spot no matter what you do, the slightly worn dish rack, the belt with extra holes punched with an ice pick that you borrowed from your cousin for exactly this purpose, the flashlight in the pantry that has never had batteries and never will, that the thought of *tired* being both your daily bread and also grounds for divorce gives me the willies. The shagginess of things, the way they never quite work out as planned and break down every other Tuesday, necessitating wine and foul language and duct tape and the wrong-size screw quietly hammered into place with the bottom of the garden gnome, seems to me the very essence of marriage; so if what makes a marriage work (the constant shifting of expectations and eternal parade of small surprises) is also what causes marriages to dissolve, where is it safe to stand?

Nowhere, of course. Every marriage is pregnant with divorce, every day, every hour, every minute. The second you finish reading this essay, your spouse could close the refrigerator, after miraculously finding a way to wedge the juice carton behind the milk jug, and call it quits, and the odd truth of the matter is that because she might end your marriage in a moment, and you might end hers, you're still married. The instant there is no chance of death is the moment of death.

Lost Dog Creek

Our creek rises at the top of a serious little hill to the west and slides all the way down into the lake below. In the summer it's a trickle and in the winter it's a bigger trickle. Only once that I remember did it get big enough to drown anything, which it did, a beaver, although I think maybe the beaver was hit by a car first, as it was not only bedraggled when we found it but much flatter than your usual beaver. My children and I were going to bury the beaver but by the time we came back with beaver-burying implements the beaver was gone. I think maybe it washed down into the lake, which feeds a massive river to the east, which feeds a massive river to the north, which feeds the Pacific Ocean, which is really massive.

No one knows what the Tualatin people who lived here called the creek, and the white people who lived here didn't write down what they called it until 1974, when the mayor, my friend Herald, had to file a resource inventory with the state of Oregon, which he did, naming unnamed or lost-named features like little creeks where beavers occasionally get drowned. Herald used to lose his dogs there so he called it Lost Dog Creek, which is its official name on maps and such now, but I have small children and they like to name things and at the moment one son calls it Squished Beaver Creek and another son calls it Found Dog Creek and my daughter calls it Not A Creek because most of the time it doesn't have water in it.

The thing is, though, that when they ask me what I want to name the creek I don't have words for the names I want to name it. I want to name it the way it mumbles and mutters in late fall. Or the gar-

136

gly word it says after a month of rain. Or all the names of the colors it is. Or the deer-language names of the two deer we saw there once. Or the *bip-bip-bip* sound the deer made when they bounded away. Or the sluggish murkish sound of people dumping motor oil in it. Or a really long name like how long it's been creeking. Or the first words of all the prayers prayed there. Or the plopping sound chestnuts make when they rain into the creek every fall. Or the sound of the bamboos sucking creek water day and night like skinny green drunks. Or the whirring song of the water ouzel we once saw there. Or the wet scuttly sound of crawdads tail-flipping away from kids wading and the screechy sound of the same kids scuttling away from the crawdads. Or the whinnying of the million robins there. Or the name of the first human who ever drank from the creek. Or the proper word for the prickly pride of the old lady who lives in the moist basement of the cement house above the creek who says her husband's on vacation but he's actually been gone for ten years. Or the sound that the creek doesn't make when there's no water in it. Or the sound that a kid down the street made right after she learned how to walk and she wobbled all the way down the street holding her mama's pinky and when she teetered past the creek she looked at it amazed and said an amazed word that no one ever said before and maybe no one ever will again and the word fell tumbling end over end into the creek and away it went to the lake and to the river and to the next river and to the ocean where everything goes eventually.

But I bet someday the word will come back. I bet one day a woman will be walking along the creek and when her child asks the name of the creek the mother will open her mouth and inside her will still be the kid down the street she once was and out will come the name of the creek again, salty and wet and amazed.

Raptorous

I have been so hawk-addled and owl-absorbed and falcon-haunted and eagle-maniacal since I was a little kid that it was a huge shock to me to discover that there were people who did *not* think that seeing a sparrow hawk helicoptering over an empty lot and then dropping like an anvil and o my god *coming up with wriggling lunch* was the coolest thing ever. I mean, who could possibly not be awed by a tribe whose various members can see a rabbit clearly from a mile away (eagles), fly sideways through tree branches like feathered fighter jets (woodhawks), look like tiny brightly colored linebackers (kestrels, with their cool gray helmets), hunt absolutely silently on the wing (owls), fly faster than any other being on earth (falcons), and can spot a trout from fifty feet in the air, gauge piscine speed and direction, and nail the dive and light-refraction and wind-gust and trout-startle so perfectly that it snags three fish a day (our friend the osprey)? Not to mention they *look* cool, they are seriously large, they have muscles on their muscles, they are stone-cold efficient hunters with built-in butchery tools, and all of them have this stern *I could kick your ass but I'm busy* look, which took me years to discover was not a general simmer of surliness but a result of the supraorbital ridge protecting their eyes.

And they are more *adamant* than other birds. They arrest your attention. You see a hawk and you stop what minor crime you are committing and pay close attention to a craft master who commands the horizon until he or she is done and drifts airily away, terrifying the underbrush. You see an eagle, you gape; you hear the piercing whistle of an osprey along the river, you stand motionless and listen with

138

reverence; you see an owl launch at dusk, like a burly gray dream against the last light, you flinch a little, and are awed, and count yourself blessed.

They inspire fear, too—that should be said. They carry switchblades and know how to use them, they back down from no one, and there are endless stories of eagles carrying away fawns and foals and kittens and cubs left unattended for a fateful moment in meadows and clearings, and falcons shearing off the eyebrows of idiots climbing to their nests, and owls casually biting off the fingers of people who discover Fluffy is actually ferocious. A friend of mine from the Oregon forest tells of watching a gyrfalcon descend upon his chickens and grab one with a daggered fist as big as my friend's fist but with much better weaponry, then rise easily into the fraught and holy air while, reports my friend with grudging admiration, the bird glared at him with the clear and inarguable message, *I am taking this chicken and you are not going to be a fool and mess with me.*

I suppose what I am talking about here is awe and reverence and some kind of deep thrumming respect for beings who are very good at what they do and fit into this world with remarkable sinewy grace. We are all hunters in the end, bruised and battered and broken in various ways, and we seek always to rise again, and fit deftly into the world, and soar to our uppermost reaches, enduring with as much grace as we can. Maybe the reason that so many human beings are as hawk-addled and owl-absorbed and falcon-haunted and eagle-maniacal as me is because we wish to live like them, to use them like stars to steer by, to remember to be as alert and unafraid as they are. Maybe being raptorous is in some way rapturous. Maybe what the word *rapture* really means is an attention so ferocious that you see the miracle of the world as the miracle it is. Maybe that is what happens to saints and mystics who float up into the air and soar beyond sight and vanish finally into the glare of the sun.

An Leabharlann

One time I was in Connemara, that tiny remnant of the Gaelic kingdom that once ruled all the green rocky sprawl of the Irish island, when I finished the books I had brought to read while traveling, and realized, with a start, that I was well and truly screwed as regards reading material, for I had already read the books my companions had, one of them twice, and the cottages where we were staying had nothing whatsoever to read, not even old magazines, so I wandered off in search of the local library.

This turned out to be a small cottage with a small librarian and a sweeping view over the sea behind it—"Bertraghboy Bay," said the tiny librarian, "which is supposed to mean *yellow sandbank* according to what's in your guide books and such, but it doesn't mean that at all, and in fact means something more like *a great place to find the oysters.* Names mean more than the words that compose them, you know. But you know that, as a literary man. No, I am afraid we do not have any of your books, but yes indeed, if you send them to me we will happily shelve them, although where to do so is a mystery at present, as you see. We are sold out, as it were, in the matter of shelf space for books, and given the parlous state of the economy, and the ruinous political management of the district, I cannot imagine that money will be miraculously found for the expansion of the library system. But having too many books is a happy problem, is it not? Because the books do wander out every day, and most of them come back. I used to be much more fidgety about retrieving them from those who kept them too long, but I gave that up years ago, on the theory that if it took some fella in Errisbeg longer than a lady in Crumpan to read such and such a book, well, then it took him longer, and as long as he did return the volume eventually, all was well. Here and there someone would lose a book, twice into the waters of the bay, but almost always a new copy would appear somehow, and to be honest it seems to me if a book goes into the bay it's a good death for the book, and surely we owe the bay a bit of thanks after all it's given us, don't you think? Not to mention there may be a well-educated lobster tribe down there, and good for them.

"How did I become a librarian? Well, now, I'll tell you, and it's a strange bit of a story, for I think it all began with the very word itself. I was just a bit of a boy with not a word of the imperial English in my head when my grandfather first took me to the library. It wasn't this building, no, it was a smaller one, someone's old cottage, as I re-member, and it was no bigger than two crows standing back to back. I remember as we walked up to it my grandfather said, with real respect and reverence, *an leabharlann,* which is the Irish for *the library,* and the way he said it, slowly and gravely, has never left my ear. To him and so to me it was a holy word, a sacred word, a crucial word. Your library is where the community stores its treasures. It's the house that imagination built. It's where all the stories that matter are gathered to-gether and celebrated and shared. It's exactly like a church, it seems to me. People come to it communally for something that's deep and ancient and important beyond an easy explanation. Who you are as a town is in the library. It's why when you want to destroy a place you burn down the library. People who fear freedom fear libraries. The urge to ban a book is always an urge to put imagination in jail. But in the end you cannot imprison it, just as you cannot imprison the urge to freedom, because those things are in every soul, and there are too many souls to jail or murder them all, and that's a fact. So a library is a shout of defiance too, if you think about it: *dorn in aghaidh an dorchadas,* a fist against the dark."

The Bullet

Here's a story. A man who was a soldier in the American army in Iraq tells it to me. A friend of his, one of his best and closest friends, was nearly pierced through by a bullet fired by a sniper. The bullet entered the friend's upper right chest, just below the collarbone, and plowed almost through to the back, just below the shoulder blade. American surgeons removed the bullet and discovered it was a 5.56-millimeter cartridge manufactured in Lake City, Missouri. The Lake City Ammunition Plant was founded by the Remington Arms Company in 1941. Today it is operated by Orbital Alliant Techsystems, which averages five billion dollars in sales annually and earns an average of about half a billion dollars annually. Half of the one hundred biggest weapons and ammunition manufacturers in the world are American companies. Orbital is one of these. Orbital sells 1.5 billion rounds of ammunition a year to the American army and to the armies of other nations around the world. Some of that ammunition is lost or stolen or shuffled clandestinely to all sorts of revolutionaries, criminals, gangs, and thugs, including some that call themselves freedom fighters or insurgents against economic and cultural imperialism, though in many cases they are actually fighting to impose their own chosen form of oppression and tinny empire on the people they live among, people whom they are not averse to slaughtering for advertising reasons.

So let us review: an American soldier, age twenty-two, is nearly pierced by a bullet made in America, sold for a profit in America by an American company that makes half a billion dollars a year selling bullets and other weaponry to armies all over the world. The vast majority of the companies that make a tremendous profit every year selling bullets and weaponry all over the world are American. Most of them are publicly traded companies in which many other Americans are heavily invested. So the bullet that nearly pierced an American boy, a bullet that caused him enormous pain, a bullet that permanently affected the use of his arm and shoulder, the bullet that cut a scar on his chest he will wear until the day he dies, was made in America, by American workers, and paid for by American investors who profited handsomely by the sale of the bullet that executed its purpose by punching a hole the size of a quarter almost all the way through a boy from America.

A 5.56-millimeter bullet can penetrate fifteen to twenty inches through "soft tissue"—*soft tissue* meaning, for example, a boy. The bullet is "prone to yaw," which means that it skews easily from a direct path, and it is also liable to fragment at what is called the cannelure, a groove around the cylinder. When a bullet fragments on delivery, the fragments slice and tear and rip and shred everything in their path, including bone. A 5.56-millimeter bullet can punch nearly half an inch into steel, and punch right through a bulletproof vest, and punch right through a human being of any size and shape and age and nationality and gender and religion and sexual orientation and combatant status, or not.

Rarely does a writer speak bluntly, ahead of time, to people who will type furious outraged insults in the comment section, after his article is posted, but I will here and now.

Dear outraged shrieking lunatic, you who are about to lecture me on how this was just an accident, and how it's a necessary part of the capitalist system, and how I am clearly a yellow liberal pansy: Are you only stupid, or are you insane? What part of all this makes sense? What part of all this is not about profit? Why should America be the biggest weapons dealer on earth? Why do we lie about how this is directly linked to murders all over the world, and how our own kids suffer and die from American weapons and ammunition? Is profit share more important than the lives of uncountable thousands of people all over the world who die from our weapons and ammunition? Are there no other products that all those American employees could possibly design and manufacture? Really? Have you ever been nearly pierced through by a 5.56-millimeter bullet? No? Then how do you have the unmitigated gall to say anything to me, you pompous ass?

Fishering

In the woods here in Oregon there is a creature that eats squirrels like candy, can kill a pursuing dog in less than a second, and is in the habit of deftly flipping over porcupines and scooping out the meat as if the prickle-pig were merely a huge and startled breakfast melon.

This riveting creature is the fisher, a member of the mustelid family that includes weasels, otter, mink, badger, ferrets, marten, and—at the biggest and most ferocious end of the family —wolverine. Sometimes called the pekan or fisher-cat, the fisher can reach three feet long, tail included, and weigh up to twelve pounds. Despite its stunning speed and agility, it is best known not as an extraordinary athlete of the thick woods and snowfields, but as the bearer of a coat so dense and lustrous that it has been sought eagerly by trappers for thousands of years—one reason the fisher is so scarce pretty much everywhere it used to live.

Biologist friends of mine tell me that Oregon has only two "significant" populations of fisher: One in the Siskiyou Mountains in the southwest, and the other in the Cascade Mountains south of Crater Lake. All the rare sightings of fisher in Oregon in recent years have been in these two areas. In the northwest coastal woods where I occasionally walk, biologists tell me firmly, there are no fishers and there have been none for more than 50 years.

I am a guy who wanders around looking for nothing in particular, which is to say everything. In this frame of mind I have seen many things, in venues urban, suburban, and rural. While ambling in the woods I have seen marten kits and three-legged elk and secret beds of watercress and the subtle dens of foxes. I have found thickets of wild grapevines, and hidden jungles of salmonberries, and stands of huckleberries so remote and so delicious that it is a moral dilemma for me as to whether or not I should leave a map behind for my children when the time comes for me to add to the compost of the world.

Suffice it to say that I have been much graced in these woods, but to see a fisher was not a gift I expected. Yet recently I found loose quills on a path, and then the late owner of the quills, with his or her conqueror atop the carcass staring at me.

I do not know if the fisher had ever seen a human being before. It evinced none of the usual sensible caution of the wild creature confronted with *Homo violencia,* and it showed no inclination whatsoever to retreat from its prize. We stared at each other for a long moment and then I sat down, thinking that a reduction of my height and a gesture of repose might send the signal that I was not dangerous, and had no particular interest in porcupine meat. Plus, I'd remembered that a fisher can slash a throat in less than a second.

Long minutes passed. The fisher fed, cautiously. I heard thrushes and wrens. I made no photographs or recordings, and when the fisher decided to evanesce I did not take casts of its tracks or claim the former porcupine as evidence of fisherness. I just watched and listened and now I tell you. I don't have any heavy message to share. I was only a witness: where there are no fishers, there was a fisher. It was a stunning creature, alert, attentive, accomplished, unafraid. And I think maybe there is much where we think there is nothing. Where there are no fishers, there was a fisher. Remember that.

Tyee

I have been writing too many condolence letters lately. I am using the same sorts of words and the words have become husks of what they used to be. Like the people I am writing about. Who are there on the page, illusory but adamant. Good thing for ritual. How else could we say anything without saying anything? Could it be that most of what we say aims at something other than what we say? Could that be? We use words so casually, such flow and fluidity and panache, but what we want to say are the rocks in the stream, the occasional brilliant bird, the serpentine mink, the lugubrious heron, the drowned ancient fungus-riddled salmon. I am writing about *tyee,* the great chinook, the king of fish, and he held adamant behind a boulder for a while as he began to dissolve and now his time has come and he slips away and I type this to his widow using words like *my most sincere sorrows,* and she knows and I know what I mean. But, for a moment, all I see on the page is the weary dignity holding in the pool.

Everyone Thinks That Awful Comes
by Itself, But It Doesn't

Iknow a guy whose wife fell in love with another man. She told him
about it first thing in the morning on a summer day. She then went
to start the coffee.

What did you do? I asked.

Just lay abed, he said, listening to her puttering in the kitchen.
Everyone thinks that awful comes by itself, but it doesn't. It comes
hand in hand with normal. No one talks about this. You're watching the basketball game when the phone rings and you find out
your grandfather didn't wake up this morning. At the scene of the
terrible car crash there's a baseball glove that fell out of one of
the cars. The awful is inside the normal. Like normal is pregnant
with awful. We know this, but we don't talk about it. A guy has
a stroke at his desk, but no one knows because he has the door
closed, which everyone takes as a sign he's on an important call. I
just lay abed. It wasn't heavy, like I couldn't move or anything. It
wasn't dramatic. I was just listening. She got the coffee ready and I
shuffled out and we had coffee and didn't say anything. No words
came to mind. That's another thing no one says—that when you
are completely shocked and horrified and broken and aghast, you
don't actually rage and weep and storm around the house. Or at
least I didn't. Maybe some people do. But I don't think so. I think
probably most people are like me and just continue along, doing
what they were going to do. I took a shower and got dressed and
went to work. My brother says I must have been in shock, but I
don't know about that. I mean, I was shocked, sure I was. But I

think it's more that there had been a terrible car crash and I was noticing the normal. It was a Saturday, so the kids were sleeping in. I go to work on Saturdays, so I went to work. Lovely day, one of those days when you see dragonflies all day long. Dragonflies are very cool. People think you look for metaphors after something like that, but I think we just keep walking. That's what I think. I mean, of course I thought about stuff like should we get divorced and how could she fall in love with another guy and how come she fell out of love with me, but mostly I thought about the kids. Sometimes I thought about the other guy, but not so much. I did wonder if we could ever get it together again, but not too much. I went to the bank and to pick up a suit at the tailor. I had a hard few moments there, because the tailor gave me an envelope with the stuff that had been in my suit pockets. This was my best suit, so I wore it for dates and weddings and wakes. There were a couple of Mass cards from funerals and wedding invites, but also there were two tampons just in case she needed them, and a photo of us at a wedding on the beach, and a ring our daughter had given me, one of those rings that you can make whistle. That ring nailed me. You would think it would be the photo of us beaming on the beach, but it was the ring.

A soldier friend of mine tells me the same thing happens when you are in a fight: that everything's normal, and then it isn't, and then it's normal again, except if there are guys screaming or crumpled and not screaming. You get up cautiously from where you are kneeling, and you look around, and everything's just like it was a minute ago, coffee and dragonflies and the kids sleeping in, and then you just keep moving. It's sort of boring, I guess, from a certain perspective.

The Four Gospels

The first time I ever entered the tiny subterranean apartment of the woman who would eventually marry me, I was struck by a number of things: her large and not especially friendly dog, who regarded me with understandable suspicion; the lack of any extraneous furniture or appurtenances other than those required by an artist who was also a superb cook; and her one small rickety bookshelf, perched over her bed, so that she could reach up with one hand, while supine, and haul down an inky companion, therein to ramble and plumb.

Being a writer, I went right to the bookshelf, which was also blessedly away from the grim and gimlet-eyed dog, and examined her collection. There were four books and four books only, although I later discovered she was a ferocious and omnivorous reader; she later explained that her days were so crammed with work and school that if she had a few moments to read at night she counted herself lucky, and these four books were, perhaps, talismans of a sort, touchstones, compass points, lodestars, old friends, necessary and nutritious companions.

I remember them well, I remember how they leaned on each other there on the incredibly rickety shelf (the whole apartment was like that, and I felt like an unruly giant whose slightest misstep or sneeze would bring tables and shelves crashing to the floor), and I report with a smile that she still owns all four of the books, though now they are surrounded by many other books, for we have been married for nearly thirty years, and our collections long ago merged and mixed and mingled, and now Ellen Gilchrist rubs up against Bernard DeVoto, and Peter Matthiessen shoulders Laurie Colwin, and Annie Dillard is cheek by jowl with Alberto Giacometti, and other interesting pairings like that, making you wonder what riveting conversations are had on the shelves at night, when all is otherwise still until Joseph Conrad begins whispering to Elinor Lipman...

The four were Willa Cather's fine *Song of the Lark,* and Harper Lee's perfect *To Kill a Mockingbird,* and David James Duncan's great headlong Pacific Northwest coming-of-age novel *The River Why,* and best of all, greatest of all, the glorious hilarious epic sprawling wondrous novel *The Horse's Mouth,* by the Irishman Joyce Cary, and that was all, just those four, the three lean and the one thick with Cary's word-wizardry; and now I look back through the years at that shelf and wonder if those four books did not nearly encapsulate and characterize and explain and draw a collective map to the woman who married me.

There was a Northwest classic, filled with burling rivers and dense spruce forests and laughter and love and confusion and epiphany and rain; and those are her things, her place, her scent. There was the story of an American woman rising to be a terrific artist, and realizing that she could steer her own life, and not be beholden to a lover or a husband or the harness, however pleasant, of family; and this is her lifelong work and story. There is the story of a bright brave American girl and a beloved stalwart father, who teaches integrity and grace by his very being; and that is her story, and her father. And there is the novel I love above all others, filled with humor and struggle and prickly grace and a yearning to marshal color and shape and paint and canvas in such ways as to sing and celebrate the entire universe and everything in it; and that is her life and work and story, as I have had many occasions to see.

I am sure she did not choose those four books as a message to such amorous suitors as me; I am sure she did not herself consider that they might collectively say something piercing and eloquent about she who owned them, and gathered them together like a musical quartet on that most rickety of shelves; but it seems to me now that amazingly they did and do speak clearly and penetratingly of she who carried them from one ocean to another, many years ago, and occasionally reached up behind her head with one hand, when she was supine and weary, and hauled down a friend, who spoke to her of character and courage, grace and humor, love and imagination, rain and affection, and so much more. Those are very good books on their own merits, but to me, and I believe to my lovely bride, they will always be great books for other reasons, some of them too subtle for words.

God

By purest chance I was out in our street when the kindergarten
Bus mumbled past going slow and I looked up just as all seven
Kids on my side of the bus looked at me and I grinned and they
Lit up and all this crap about God being dead and where is God
And who owns God and who hears God better than whom is the
Most egregiously stupid crap imaginable because if you want to
See God and have God see you and have this mutual perception
Be completely untrammeled by blather and greed and comment,
Go stand in the street as the kindergarten bus murmurs past. I'm
Not kidding and this is not a metaphor. I am completely serious.
Everyone babbles about God but I saw God this morning just as
The bus slowed down for the stop at Maple Street. God was six
Girls and one boy with a bright green and purple stegosaurus hat.
Of course God would wear a brilliantly colored tall dinosaur hat!
If you were the Imagination that dreamed up everything that ever
Was in this blistering perfect terrible world, wouldn't you wear a
Hat celebrating some of the wildest most amazing developments?

V.

We Are Better Than
We Think

Clairtonica Street

Our dad never spoke about his childhood at all when
We were kids. We would ask him and he would chat
About this and that and the other thing; we were easy
To distract, and Dad was gentle and funny and to hear
Him on any subject was a pleasure. Many years went
By, and then the sons decided to haul him back to his
Native Pittsburgh. We were checking genealogy. But
When we drove up a snowy hill, and found the house
He had lived in as a child, he burst into tears. We had
Never seen Dad cry before, none of us. We sat quietly.
My brothers and our father are big tall guys and there
Was a sort of long big tall quiet in the van. Very large
Men being silent is a *sound*. Good thing no one spoke.
Any words right then would have been a sort of insult.
We could talk, afterward, about how our father opened
The gates and told us everything, all the pain and loss,
All the ways he created his gentle quiet wry manhood,
All the wit and dignity and love and patience and guts,
All the ways his life was a song of grace and gratitude.
But for now let's just sit here in the back of the old van.
Give the man time with his tears. He waited something
Like seventy years to cry these tears. You have to give
These tears some space and some respect. In a moment
He'll say, gentle as always, *that's my house! my house!*,
But now let's just sit and revere him from the back seat.

Dawn and Mary

Early one morning several teachers and staffers at a Connecticut grade school were in a meeting. The meeting had been underway for about five minutes when they heard a chilling sound in the hallway. (We heard pop-pop-pop, said one of the staffers later.)

Most of them dove under the table. That is the reasonable thing to do, what they were trained to do, and that is what they did.

But two of the staffers jumped, or leaped, or lunged out of their chairs and ran toward the sound of bullets. Which word you use depends on which news account of that morning you read, but the words all point in the same direction—toward the bullets.

One of the staffers was the principal. Her name was Dawn. She had two daughters. Her husband had proposed to her five times before she'd finally said yes, and they had been married for ten years. They had a vacation house on a lake. She liked to get down on her knees to paint with the littlest kids in her school.

The other staffer was a school psychologist named Mary. She had two daughters. She was a football fan. She had been married for more than thirty years. She and her husband had a cabin on a lake. She loved to go to the theater. She was due to retire in one year. She liked to get down on her knees to work in her garden.

Dawn the principal told the teachers and the staffers to lock the door behind them, and the teachers and the staffers did so after Dawn and Mary ran out into the hall.

You and I have been in that hallway. We spent seven years of our childhood in that hallway. It's friendly and echoing, and when someone opens the doors at the end, a wind comes and flutters all the paintings and posters on the walls.

Dawn and Mary jumped, or leaped, or lunged toward the sound of bullets. Every fiber of their bodies—bodies descended from millions of years of bodies that had leaped away from danger—must have wanted to dive under the table. That's what they'd been trained to do. That's how you live to see another day. That's how you stay alive to paint with the littlest kids and work in the garden and hug your daughters and drive off laughing to your cabin on the lake.

But they leaped for the door, and Dawn said, *Lock the door after us,* and they lunged right at the boy with the rifle.

The next time someone says the word *hero* to you, you say this:
There once were two women. One was named Dawn, and the other was named Mary. They both had two daughters. They both loved to kneel down to care for small beings. They leaped from their chairs and ran right at the boy with the rifle, and if we ever forget their names, if we ever forget the wind in that hallway, if we ever forget what they did, if we ever forget that there is something in us beyond sense and reason that snarls at death and runs roaring at it to defend children, if we ever forget that all children are our children, then we are fools who have allowed memory to be murdered too, and what good are we then? What good are we then?

His Last Game

We were supposed to be driving to the pharmacy for his prescriptions, but he said just drive around for a while, my prescriptions aren't going anywhere without me, so we just drove around. We drove around the edges of the college where he had worked and we saw a blue heron in a field of stubble, which is not something you see every day, and we stopped for a while to see if the heron was fishing for mice or snakes, on which we bet a dollar, me taking mice and him taking snakes, but the heron glared at us and refused to work under scrutiny, so we drove on. We drove through the arboretum checking on the groves of ash and oak and willow trees, which were still where they were last time we looked, and then we checked on the wood-duck boxes in the pond, which still seemed sturdy and did not feature ravenous weasels that we noticed, and then we saw a kestrel hanging in the crisp air like a tiny helicopter, but as soon as we bet mouse or snake the kestrel vanished, probably for religious reasons, said my brother, probably a lot of kestrels are adamant that gambling is immoral, but we are just not as informed as we should be about kestrels.

We drove deeper into the city and I asked him why we were driving this direction, and he said I am looking for something that when I see it you will know what I am looking for, which made me grin, because he knew and I knew that I would indeed know, because we have been brothers for 50 years, and brothers have many languages, some of which are physical, like broken noses and fingers and teeth and punch-

160

ing each other when you want to say *I love you* but don't know how to say that right, and some of them are laughter, and some of them are roaring and spitting, and some of them are weeping in the bathroom, and some of them we don't have words for yet. By now it was almost evening, and just as I turned on the car's running lights I saw what it was he was looking for, which was a basketball game in a park. I laughed and he laughed and I parked the car. There were six guys on the court and to their credit they were playing full court. Five of the guys looked to be in their twenties, and they were fit and muscled, and one of them wore a porkpie hat. The sixth guy was much older, but he was that kind of older ballplayer who is comfortable with his age and he knew where to be and what not to try. We watched for a while and didn't say anything but both of us noticed that one of the young guys was not as good as he thought he was, and one was better than he knew he was, and one was flashy but essentially useless, and the guy with the porkpie hat was a worker, setting picks, boxing out, whipping outlet passes, banging the boards not only on defense but on offense, which is much harder. The fifth young guy was one of those guys who ran up and down yelling and waving for the ball, which he never got. This guy was supposed to be covering the older guy but he didn't bother, and the older guy gently made him pay for his inattention, scoring occasionally on backdoor cuts and shots from the corners on which he was so alone he could have opened a circus and sold tickets, as my brother said. The older man grew visibly weary as we watched, and my brother said he's got one last basket in him, and I said I bet a dollar it's a shot from the corner, and my brother said no, he doesn't even have the gas for that, he'll snake the kid somehow, you watch, and just then the older man, who was bent over holding the hems of his shorts like he was exhausted, suddenly cut to the basket, caught a bounce pass, and scored, and the game ended, maybe because the park lights didn't go on even though the streetlight did.

On the way home my brother and I passed the heron in the field of stubble again, and the heron stopped work again and glared at us until we turned the corner. That is one withering glare, said my brother. That's a ballplayer glare if ever I saw one. That's the glare a guy gives another guy when the guy you were supposed to be covering scores on a backdoor cut and you thought your guy was ancient and near death but it turns out he snaked you good and you are an idiot. I know that glare. You owe me a dollar. We better go get my prescriptions. They are not going to do any good but we better get them anyway so they don't go to waste. One less thing for my family to do afterward. That game was good but the heron was even better. I think the prescriptions are pointless now but we already paid for them so we might as well get them. They'll just get thrown out if we don't pick them up. That was a good last game, though. I'll remember the old guy, sure, but the kid with the hat banging the boards, that was cool. You hardly ever see a guy with a porkpie hat hammering the boards. There's so much to love, my brother added. All the little things. Remember shooting baskets at night and the only way you could tell if the shot went in was the sound of the net? Remember the time we cut the fingertips off our gloves so we could shoot on icy days and Dad was so angry he lost his voice and he was supposed to give a speech and had to gargle and Mom laughed so hard we thought she was going to pee? Remember that? I remember that. What happens to what I remember? You remember it for me, okay? You remember the way that heron glared at us like he would kick our ass except he was working. And you remember that old man snaking that kid. Stupid kid, you could say, but that's the obvious thing. The beautiful thing is the little thing that the old guy knew full well he wasn't going to cut around picks and drift out into the corner again, that would burn his last gallon of gas, not to mention he'd have to hoist up a shot from way out there, so he snakes the kid beautiful, he knows the kid thinks he's old, and the guy with the hat sees him cut, and gets him the ball on a dime, that's a beautiful thing because it's little, and we saw it and we knew what it meant. You remember that for me. You owe me a dollar.

Memorial Day

We are at a parade. It is Memorial Day. I am sitting on the curb in front of the church with my brother, reserving our family's spot. The rest of the family is coming along slowly, our father carrying the baby, but my brother and I have run ahead because we don't want to miss a single soldier in uniform or girl twirling a baton or bespectacled beaming cherubic man wearing a fez. We might see an elephant. We will see horses and fire trucks. We will see politicians in convertibles. We will see men older than our dad wearing their Army uniforms. Army is green and the others are blue. Our dad will not walk in the parade wearing his uniform. He declines politely every year when he is asked. He says he no longer has his uniform. He says he does not know where it went, although we think he does know where it went. He says he wore it only because the job had to be done, and now that the war is over, there is no reason to have a uniform. He says uniforms are dangerous statements, if you think about it. He says uniforms can easily confer false authority, and encourage hollow bravado, and augment unfortunate inclinations, and exacerbate violent predilections. This is how he talks. He says uniforms are public pronouncements, like parades, and we should be careful about what we say in public. He says we should be leery of men marching in uniforms. He says no one has more respect for members of the armed forces than he does, but that it would be a better world if no one ever had to take up arms, and that is a fact. He says in his experience it is the man who has been in a war who understands that war is cruel and foolish and sinful, and anyone who defends war as natural to the human condition is a person of stunted imagination. He says a study of history shows not only that we are a savage species but that we are a species capable of extraordinary imaginative leaps. He says that someday we might devise ways to *outwit* violence, as Mr. Mohandas Gandhi tried to do. He says most wars, maybe all wars, are about money in the end, and that when we hear the beating of war drums, we should suspect that it is really a call for market expansion. He says war is a virus and imagination is the cure.

Our father does not have his uniform anymore, but he does have a wooden box in a drawer in his bureau at home. There are medals and service bars and ribbons in the box. We have secretly opened the box, my brother and I, and handled its contents, and put them back exactly the way we found them, so that he would not know, but he knows. His photographs are in another drawer. In them he is tall and thin and shockingly young. He is a private, a sergeant, a lieutenant. He is on Bougainville Island in the South Pacific. Then he is in the Philippines. He is preparing for the invasion of Japan. He is preparing to die.

Today he is standing next to us at the Memorial Day parade as the soldiers and sailors pass by. Some men in the crowd salute, but he does not. He keeps his eyes locked on the soldiers, though, even as we are pulling at his hands and pant legs and the baby is crying and wriggling. The one time he hands off the baby and applauds quietly is when the firemen pass by in their trucks. After the firemen come the Girl Scouts and Boy Scouts, and the Little League baseball play-ers, and the Knights of Columbus, and the Rotary Club, and finally a visiting fife-and-drum corps from Ireland, and then we walk home, our dad carrying the baby, who fell asleep just after the Girl Scouts walked by.

100th Street

By chance I was in New York City seven months after September 11, and I saw a moment that I still turn over and over in my mind like a puzzle, like a koan, like a prism.

I had spent the day at a conference crammed with uninformed opinions and droning speeches and stern lectures, and by the evening I was weary of it all, weary of being sermonized by pompous authority, weary of the cocksure and the arrogant and the tin-eared, weary of what sold itself as deeply religious but was actually grim moral policing with not the slightest hint of mercy or humility in the air, and I slipped out and away from the prescribed state dinner, which promised only more speeches and lectures.

I was way up on the upper west side of the Island of the Manhattoes, near the ephemeral border of Harlem, and as I was in the mood to walk off steam, I walked far and wide; down to the Sailors and Soldiers Monument, by the vast Hudson River, and up to Joan of Arc Park, with Joan on her rearing charger, and up to the Firemen's Memorial on 100th Street. I thought about wandering up to the great old castle church of Saint John the Divine on 111th Street but by now I was footsore and yearning for beer and I stepped into a bar.

It was that russet hour between evening and night and the bar was populous but not crowded. Most of the people seemed to have stopped by for a beer after work. One table of men in the corner wore the faded coveralls of telephone linemen or public utility workers. Another table of mature women were in the bland dark uniforms of corporate staff. Interestingly there was a young Marine in glittering full dress uniform at the bar, with two older men I took to be his father and uncle, perhaps; they were laughing and resting their hands affectionately on his shoulders and he was smiling and savoring their hands like they were pet birds he had not had on his shoulders for a long time.

I got a beer and sat in the corner and watched as the bartender, who wore a lovely old-style long bowtie, set a beer in front of the Marine and waved off the uncle's offer to pay, and his little cheerful gesture made me happy, and I concluded that this would be the gentle tender respectful highlight of a day in which there had been very little respect and tenderness, but then the door opened, and two young firemen walked in. They were not in full dress uniform but they had their FDNY shirts on, and I noticed their sturdy work boots, and somehow you could tell that they were firemen and not just guys who happened to be wearing FDNY shirts.

They took a few steps toward the bar, and then something happened that I will never forget. Everyone in the bar stood up, silently. The table of women stood up first, I noticed, and then everyone else stood up, including me. I thought perhaps someone would start to applaud but no one made a sound. The men standing at the bar turned and faced the firemen, and then the young Marine drew himself up straight as a tree and saluted the firemen, and then his father and uncle saluted too, and then everyone else in the bar saluted the firemen. I tell you that there wasn't a sound in the place, not the clink of a glass or the shuffle of feet or a cough or anything.

After a few seconds one of the firemen nodded to everyone, and the other fireman made a slight gesture of acknowledgement with his right hand, and the bartender set two beers on the bar, and everyone sat down again, and everything went on as before; but not.

God Again

Had a brief chat with God the other day. This was at the United States Post Office. God was manning the counter from one to five, as he does every blessed day. He actually says *every blessed day* and he means it. You never saw a more patient being. He never loses his cool and believe me he could. I would. I have been in line behind crazies at his window and heard vituperative abuse and vulgar character assassination and scurrilous insinuation and never once did I witness any flash of temper in response to this on his part. I have asked him how he could maintain his cool and he says things like *I try to put myself in their position* and *Witnessing vented emotion is part of the job* and *All storms blow over* and *It's only frustration* and *There are so many much more serious things* and *We are all neighbors in the end.* I am impressed by these sentiments, in large part because I share them consistently in theory but inconsistently in practice. God, however, does not waver nor does he fluctuate in his equanimity. He stands there quietly as people bang their fists on his counter and offer rude remarks and stomp away muttering darkly. He does not smile when someone gets upset. He says he has learned that some people get more upset if you smile when they are upset. He listens to what they say and often, I notice, he makes a note on a pad as they leave. *I make a note if I think they have a good point we should discuss with management,* he says. *Often what is couched as a complaint is actually a good point about how we could be of better service.* He remembers pretty much every regular who comes to his window and he greets them politely by name. Sometimes he will inquire after children and animals. Dogs

167

adore God and will sometimes rear up on his counter to see him better. He greets them politely by name surprisingly often. *I would guess I know a hundred dogs by name*, he says. *Hardly any cats. People don't take their cats with them when they go to the Post Office.* I make a joke about how cats are the children of Lucifer and he does not smile and I realize later that probably Lucifer is still a deeply sad and touchy subject for him. How would *you* feel if one of your best friends, one of your most trusted companions, tried to steal everything you had and were and did, and for this breathtaking betrayal he was cast shrieking into the darkness, no longer the Shining One, the Morning Star, but the very essence of squirming withered despair, until the end of time? Wouldn't you be haunted and sad about that ever after? I would. I felt bad and told God I was sorry about making a stupid joke. I said I made stupid jokes all the time even though I was now an older citizen and ought to have learned by now to not be so flippant. And God said, *No worries,* and *Better a poor joke than something worse,* and *Do you want to use the book rate for your package, which will save you about five bucks?* And I said yes, sir, and thank you, and walked out of the Post Office thinking that if we cannot see God in the vessels into which the electricity of astonishing life is poured by a profligate creation, vessels like this wonderfully and eternally gracious gentleman at the Post Office, then we are very bad at the religion we claim to practice, which says forthrightly that God is everywhere available, if only we remove the beam from our eyes, and bow in humility and gratitude for the miraculous, which falleth even as the light from the sun, which touches all beings, and is withheld from none. So it is that I have seen God at the United States Post Office, and spoken to him, and been edified and elevated by his grace, which slakes all those who thirst; which is each of us, which is all of us.

Beer with Peter

Twice in this life I had a beer with the great wry complicated writer, mystic, and adventurer Peter Matthiessen, and both times we ended up having more than one beer, and both times Peter ended up telling me one story after another with great high glee, and both times he finally said, *Well, I had better get going, beer on me next time.* But then Peter went and died, a year ago in April, and every couple of weeks or so, when I see his name, or see a face as craggy and ravined and humorous and weathered and amused as his, I think of his tall stooped lean grace, his lovely prose, and the fact that he owes me something like six beers, which I am never going to get in this lifetime, but hope to get later, if I have a chance to sit down with Peter again, and listen to him tell me stories with great high glee.

At dinner once with two other guests, I heard Peter explain quite seriously how he was convinced he was the direct descendant of Matthias, the 13th apostle, the one who was elected after Judas Iscariot came to an untimely end. But the times I sat and drank beer with him in Oregon, and we laughed ourselves silly, stay with me as the best times I had with Peter, and I would like to take a moment and remember those times.

He had joined the Navy in 1945, and been assigned to Hawaii, and being a bright and unprincipled young man, Peter set up a system whereby he could sell passes for the use of motor vehicles, which was not a practice approved by the Navy, although the Navy, he said, did not know about it, and perhaps still does not know about it, until now. He also set up baseball leagues for Navy personnel in Hawaii, he said, and when I asked if he had made money from that too he said no, although he had certainly thought about it, but the only way he could see to profit would be to promote cheating, and it would be a low sort of man who would cheat at baseball. He talked about his travels in Nepal and Africa and Latin America and the Antarctic; he talked about his travels in Indian Country, as he called the vast poor brave rough sad ancient lands on which so many aboriginal Americans live today; he talked about being a commercial fisherman off Long Island, which was called Paumonok by the first peoples there, he noted, and ought to be called Paumonok again, rather than Long Island, which is a remarkably unimaginative label for such a lovely place. He talked about being a Buddhist, and about his days in Paris after the war, and about his hundreds and perhaps thousands of friends among the writers and photographers and painters and poets and mystics and adventurers of the world, which in a way, as he said, is pretty much everyone, don't you think?

He talked about his beer belly, what there was of it, which he thought every man of sense ought to have after age 60 or so, or else perhaps you have been too abstemious, too penurious, too fearful of joy, as he said. He talked about his predilection for vests, which he loved for their plethora of pockets, in which you could put fishing ephemera and good pens and small notebooks and cool feathers, such as the owl feather he had the second time we met for beer.

He was a wonderful talker, a raconteur, funny and observant and memorious, and he had the great talker's gift of pausing occasionally and asking *you* questions and listening intently to you, so that your time would seem conversational, though it was much more a great storyteller patient with and amused by an apprentice storyteller; and most of all, I think, he was liable to humor, and humble enough, despite a healthy ego and sense of himself, to know very well that humor is the final frontier, that humor has something crucially to do with humility, and that humility is very probably the one inarguable mark of maturity, and whatever it is we mean when we use the word *wisdom.*

* * *

I suspect Peter had many travails and shadows in his life, most of them probably caused by or abetted by himself; I remember flashes and intimations of sadness in his talk, in his extraordinary mountainside of a face; but I will remember best and most his liability to humor, and the fact that he owes me something like six beers, which I very much hope to sip, somehow, someday, while listening to the direct descendant of the Apostle Matthias. Rest in peace, Peter; rest in the knowledge that many people remember you with affection and respect and laughter, and that millions more will read your books for centuries to come, and so meet you for themselves; perhaps, happily, while sipping beer.

The Lair

A while ago a man delivered the most stunning speech I ever heard. It was not taped and it was not delivered from a text, so there is no record of it, except in the stunned hearts of the fifty people who heard it. I have thought about his talk pretty much every day since, and I want to try to re-create it here, so that you will think about it every day, too. Perhaps then something will happen.

The man who delivered the talk is a devout Buddhist. Twice in recent years he traveled from his home in America to Auschwitz and Birkenau, the Nazi death camps in Poland. In these dark scars on the earth two million people were roasted because they were Jewish. People from all over the world now go to these camps to pray.

The man and his companions stayed in those dark scars for a week at a time, wandering through the camps, weeping, sitting for long hours in prayer, walking silent through the silent museums. Some of his companions were so oppressed by the spoor of evil that they could not rise from their beds.

One night at Auschwitz, he said, we were all gathered together in one room, more than a hundred of us, when a rabbi with us reached out with both hands and grasped the hands of the people standing next to him. Slowly most of the people in the room began to hold hands, and then they began to sway a little, and then some began to gently dance, and then, he said, there rose up in that room such a powerful joy that we were stunned and speechless and confused. Nearly every person in that room felt that sweeping joy, he said, but not everyone; several people ran out, horrified that there was dancing and joy here at the very lair of evil.

What happened that night? he asked. How could there be dancing at Auschwitz?

I do not know, he said. Help me find an answer.

When we came down from the trees sixty million years ago, he said, we were naked and slow and weak, and to survive we evolved superb brains and great ferocity and an endless thirst for killing, and that is why we kill everything, including each other. We are capable of unspeakable evil, every one of us. The Nazis are in us. No one can be at Auschwitz and not feel evil twitching in himself. It is the place where arguments end.

But, he said, what if our moral evolution sped up now as fast as our physical and intellectual evolution has? What if this is happening to many of us already? What if this evolution sometimes feels like reasonless joy? What might our world become if this is so?*

---

* The speaker was Peter Matthiessen, who told me the same story as I was driving him up the Blackfoot River to fly fish. The "rabbi" is Tetsugen Bernard Glassman, a Zen Buddhist roshi and Peter's friend. To experience joy at Auschwitz and Birkenau, Peter told me, was no laughing matter. He tried to write of it for years but couldn't find a way to do so without alienating Jewish friends. He finally solved the riddle, fearlessly, fatally, by contracting terminal cancer and spending his last months fictionalizing the experiences in his last book, the novel *In Paradise*. Peter was gracious to Jewish friends in describing the joy: he makes his protagonist's account ambiguous. *Did the joy really happen? Even if it did, might it have been some kind of desperate group hallucination?* But when Peter described his experiences on our way up the Blackfoot, there was no ambiguity. Two times, he said, turning "his extraordinary mountainside of a face" toward me so his eyes could say *I mean this,* Peter and the majority of two groups of people, after a horrendous week, were assailed by a sustained joy that moved those who didn't flee to join hands and gently dance, though only the joy itself knew why.

A Song for Nurses

The first time I saw a nurse I was four years old and someone had cut my tonsils out and I woke up addled to find a cheerful woman wearing white leaning over me and murmuring something gentle. The room was all white and the bed was all white and there were white curtains framing the window. I thought I had died and was in heaven and the woman leaning over me was an angel. I was deeply relieved to be in heaven because I had recently sinned grievously and my brother still had a black eye. For a moment I wondered if the woman smiling at me was the Madonna but then I remembered the Madonna wore blue. The woman leaning over me then said gently, everything will be all right, which it was, after a time during which I discovered that I was not dead and that she was a nurse. For me ever since nurses are essentially angelic and gentle and witty and brilliant and holy beings who bring light and peace, even though I know they must have dark nights when they are weary and sad and thrashed by despair like a beach by a tide.

I have seen nurses help bring my children out of the sea of their mother and into the sharp and bracing air of this world. I have seen nurses praying by my tiny son's bed before and after his heart was edited so that he could live to be a lanky and testy teenager today. I have seen nurses grappling cheerfully with the wires and coils and tubes and plugs and buttons and toggles and keyboards of vast machinery beyond my ken. I have seen nurses with blood on their blouses in the nether reaches of the night in emergency rooms. I have seen nurses hold my children's heads as my children were sick upon their shoes, and never a snarl did I hear from those nurses, but only a soothing sound deep in the throats, a sound far more ancient than any civilization. I have heard friends of mine who are nurses speak eloquently and articulately about their work as witness, as story-saving, as patience and endurance, as being those souls who stand by the door between life and death and usher other people through it in both directions. I have quietly gaped in awe at the sinewy courage and flinty strength and oceanic grace of nurses, and many times considered what our hospitals and hospices and clinics and schools and lives would be without them; which is to say starker and colder and more brittle and fearful. We would be even more alone and scared than we are now when faced with pain and confusion.

We take them for granted, yes we do. We think of them with reverence and gratitude only when we see them briskly and gently at work, leaning over us and those we love, being both tart and sweet at once; but here, this morning, let us pause a moment and pray for them in the holy cave of our mouths, and thank the Mercy for these most able and skillful agents of His dream for us. And let us pray not only for the extraordinary smiling armies of nurses among us; let us pray to be like them, sinewy and tender, gracious and honest, avatars of love.

Cool Things

As a fan's notes for grace, a quavery chant against the dark, I sing a song of things that make us grin and bow, that just for an instant let us see sometimes the web and weave of merciful, the endless possible, the incomprehensible inexhaustible inexplicable yes,

Such as, for example, to name a few:

The way the sun crawls over the rim of the world every morning like a child's face rising beaming from a pool all fresh from the womb of the dark, and the way jays hop and damselflies do that geometric aero-amazing thing and bees inspect and birds probe and swifts chitter, and the way the young mother at the bus stop has her infant swaddled and huddled against her chest like a blinking extra heart, and the way a very large woman wears the tiniest miniskirt with a careless airy pride that makes me so happy I can hardly squeak, and the way seals peer at me owlishly from the surf like rubbery grandfathers, and the way cormorants in the ocean never ever get caught by onrushing waves but disappear casually at the last possible second so you see their headlong black stories written on the wet walls of the sea like moist petroglyphs, and the way no pavement asphalt macadam concrete cement thing can ultimately defeat a tiny relentless green thing, and the way people sometimes lean eagerly face-first into the future, and the way infants finally discover to their absolute agogishment that those fists swooping by like tiny fleshy comets are theirs!, and the way when my mom gets caught unawares by a joke she barks with laughter so infectious that people grin two towns over, and the way one of my sons sleeps every night with his right leg hanging over the side of his bed like an oar no matter how many times I fold him back into the boat of the bed, and the way the refrigerator hums to itself in two different keys, and the way the new puppy noses through hayfields like a headlong exuberant hairy tractor, and the way my daughter always makes one immense final cookie the size of a door when she makes cookies, and the way one son hasn't had a haircut since Napoleon was emperor, and the way crows arrange themselves sometimes on the fence like the notes of a song I don't know yet, and the way car engines sigh for a few minutes after you turn them off, and the way your arm goes all totally nonchalant when you are driving through summer with the window down, and the way people touch each other's forearms when they are scared, and the way every once in a while someone you hardly know says something so piercingly honest that you want to just kneel down right there in the grocery store near the pears, and the way little children fall asleep with their mouths open like fish, and the way sometimes just a sidelong glance from someone you love makes you all shaky for a second before you can get your mask back on, and the way some people when they laugh tilt their heads way back like they need more room for all the hilarity in their mouths, and the way hawks and eagles always look so annoyed, and the way people shuffle daintily on icy pavements, and the way churches smell dense with hope, and the way that men's pants bunch up at the knees when they stand after kneeling in church, and the way knees are gnarled, and the way faces curve around the mouth and eyes according to how many times you smiled over the years, and the way people fall asleep in chairs by the fire and snap awake startled and amazed, unsure, just for a second, what planet exactly they are on, which is a question we should probably all ask far more often than we do. Look, I know very well that brooding misshapen evil is everywhere, in the brightest houses and the most cheerful denials, in what we do and what we have failed to do, and I know all too well that the story of the world is entropy, things fly apart, we sicken, we fail, we grow weary, we divorce, we are hammered and hounded by loss and accidents and tragedies. But I also know, with all my hoary muddled heart, that we are carved of immense confusing holiness; that the whole point for us is grace under duress; and that you either take a flying leap at nonsensical illogical unreasonable ideas like marriage and marathons and democracy and divinity, or you huddle behind the wall. I believe that the coolest things there are cannot be measured, calibrated, calculated, gauged, weighed, or understood except sometimes by having a child patiently explain it to you, which is another thing that should happen far more often to us all. In short I believe in believing, which doesn't make sense, which gives me hope.

Address Unknown

In the two years since my brother Kevin died one summer afternoon at age 64, I have often wanted to write to him—partly from long habit, as I wrote to him steadily for years, and partly because there continue to be many things I wish to tell him even if he can no longer open my letters.

But I did not write, having no address for him in his current form, and being unwilling to have my own letter returned to me, sad and bedraggled after a fruitless voyage; I think I would weep at that, and I have wept enough.

But I realize this morning that I can write a letter, and perhaps he can read it, if I do not mail it in traditional form, but post it in the electrosphere; for he is himself now free ions and electrons, and probably capable of apprehending and understanding matters far beyond my ken; so I sit down and begin.

Your grandson is now a year old, and rotund and hilarious, and wobbling to his feet, mostly holding on to furniture as he cruises around the room. I report with horror that his mother makes him wear bow ties at social events. I'll take care of that. The Los Angeles Lakers are incredibly awful this year and it's delicious to watch and you and I would have enjoyed every egregious minute. The tree your wife and children planted in your memory is now 15 feet tall. The wood ducks are a little late this year; it's been a hard winter. Notre Dame had a decent year in football. Your wake was hilarious, like you wanted. I still have your last message on my phone: *I worry about my kids, and will you keep an eye on them?* Whenever I see an owl I want to call you. I bet a hundred people think about you every few days, which is a cool epitaph. I saw Mom and Dad a while ago, and they told me the story again about how you didn't talk at all for your first couple of years and they were getting really worried, and then you said clear as a bell, *Is that a greenhouse?* which still makes Dad laugh. Mom and Dad are getting more fragile and papery and transparent and illuminated by the day. Bruce Springsteen has not announced he will run for president in 2016, but I have high hopes. I have been reading a great number of books about otters and badgers and foxes. The other day when I asked our dog where you were, he turned immediately to the west. I found this fascinating and was going to call but this note will have to suffice. I have to go and pick up a child now. I love you, man. Send me a postcard?

Hawk Words

The last time I saw my brother Kevin in the flesh was three years ago, in his den, in the evening, just before summer began. We sat with our legs sprawled out and talked of hawks and love and pain and Mom and beaches and mathematics and Dad and college and his children and mine and our patient, mysterious wives and books and basketball and grace and pain and then hawks again.

We were both major, serious, intent raptor guys, delighted to try to discern the difference between, say, a kestrel and a jay, which are about the same size, although one can dismember a mouse in seconds and the other would faint dead away if dismemberment was on the syllabus.

Both of us would happily have studied hawks for the rest of our lives, but the problem was that his life was ending soon, and this was the last evening we would have to talk about love and hawks, and we knew this, so we talked about hawks and love.

In my experience, brothers don't often talk bluntly about love, even if you do love each other inarticulately and thoroughly and confusedly, because it's awkward to talk about love that's not romantic. Everyone chatters and sings and gibbers about romantic love, and how it starts and ends and waxes and wanes, but we hardly ever talk about all the other kinds of love, which include affection and respect and reverence, and also brothering, which is rough and complicated.

Brothers start out in competition and some never stop. Brothers are like trees that start out adjacent but have to grow apart to eat enough light. Brothers worship each other and break each other's noses, and adore each other and steal from each other, and detest each other even as they sprint to defend each other. It's very confusing.

If you are very lucky, you eventually get to be the same age as your brother or brothers. Eventually the differences between and among you erode and dissolve and the love is left in craggy outcrops where you can sit together with your legs sprawled out.

So we talked about love, but we used hawk words. That's what I wanted to tell you this morning. We talked about how it's awfully hard to tell sharp-shinned hawks apart from Cooper's hawks and who was Cooper anyway?

We talked about the immeasurably old war between crows and red-tailed hawks, and who started that war, and why, and sure it was about a girl, sure it was.

We talked about owls and ospreys and eagles and kites and falcons and other raptors, too. But mostly we talked about hawks because we knew hawks and saw hawks every day and had always both been addled and thrilled by them and always would be even after one of us was ashes in a stone box under an oak tree.

We talked about how often you can see better with your soul than you can with your eyes in some strange deep way that I cannot explain though I've been trying to articulate the inarticulable for a long time. We talked about how one of us promised to stay addled and thrilled by hawks as long as he lived, so that both of us would still be delighted by hawks somehow. So it is that now, when I see a sharp-shinned hawk slicing sideways through oak branches at super-sonic speed in pursuit of a flitter of waxwings, my brother Kevin sees it, too, though the prevailing theory is that he is dead.

Often I find myself mumbling, "O my gawd did you see that?" and he mutters, "What could possibly be cooler than that?" and somehow we are still sprawled and lucky and it is almost summer and we are talking about love.

Bird to Bird

When I was a child my grandmother withered over the course of some months until finally she was the size of a bird. In the end she was all bones and glare. She was a hawk one day and a gull another and a heron the next depending on the light. You would go to visit her and expect to see a gull like last time but instead there would be a disgruntled osprey in the bed. I pointed this out to my mother but she did not answer. Mom went every day. She took a different child with her every day. She would just look at one of us in a certain way when it was time to go and you would get in the car, mewling. The birds in Grandmother's bed made gentle mewling noises sometimes. Sometimes Grandmother cried without any sound. It is a loud silence when someone cries without any sound. She had lived with us for years. She was stern and forbidding and brooded in her perch like an eagle. Her spectacles flashed sometimes when she looked at you. Birds can see much farther than people can. She could see through walls and around corners. She knew what you were doing before you did it. We would enter her room in the nursing home and Mom would say something gently and a falcon would open her eyes on the pillow. I wondered if the nurses knew that Grandmother could change form as she liked. Perhaps she could no longer control the changes and all day long she went from bird to bird under the sheets. That would be a tumult of birds. The nurses must have known but they probably loved birds and didn't say anything to anyone about it. Often Mom would say something gently and Grandmother would not open her eyes at all and Mom would just sit on the edge of the bed brooding and I would watch the bed for birds. Did she have a favorite bird to be? If you could be any bird would you be every bird or choose only one in which to live? Could you get stuck being a bird and forget that you were a person? Could the bird you wanted to be refuse you? Some questions you cannot ask anyone older. They will laugh or frown or give you advice. You have to just hold the question calmly in your hand and wait for the answers to come or not as they please. You cannot tell the birds what to do. The answer to a lot of questions is a bird. One time when Mom said something gently to Grandmother in the bed, an owl opened her eyes. Owls have piercing yellow eyes for which the words *entrancing* and *alluring* and *riveting* and *commanding* and *terrifying* were invented. Yellow is a dangerous color. Yellow means caution. Yellow means be careful and watch out and trouble ahead. Grandmother died very soon after that. You would not think a woman could wither into a heron but what do we know? Probably when Grandmother died the nurses picked up the heron gently and carefully and reverently in a towel and carried her outside, with prayers in their mouths, and they buried her under the sweet-gum trees. Birds love sweet-gum seeds. Probably whatever people thought Grandmother was is only a little of what she was. Surely we are made of more things than we know. We could be part goshawk, or languages no one knows anymore, or dreams a turtle had one winter under the ice. That could be. We went to Grandmother's wake because that is what our people did, and we went to the funeral because that is what our people did, but we did not go to the burial, because that is not what our people did, and also probably no one wanted to see the lean thin coffin in which you would bury a blue heron. Years later when I was driving past the nursing home where Grandmother died I thought maybe I would stop and poke under the sweet-gum trees for heron bones, but then I drove on, because I like questions better than answers. Birds are how air answers questions. Birds are languages looking for speakers. Birds are dreams you can have only if you stay awake.

To the Beach

One time for no reason at all my kid brother and I decided to ride our bicycles from our small brick house all the way to Jones Beach. We got maps out of the family car and pored over them and concluded that it was about four miles to the shore. He was twelve and I was thirteen. We could cut through a few neighborhoods before we had to thrash along in the grass on the shoulder of the highway. Riding the shoulder would be a problem because twice the highway crossed bridges over the tidal flats and we would have to dismount and balance our bikes on the six-inch curb by the rail. We figured we would worry about this when we came to it. We supplied ourselves with two cans of soda, two sandwiches, and a beach towel apiece. We debated about the surfboard. What if it was windy out on the highway and the board caught a gust and one of us was obliterated by a truck? Mom would be mad and the surviving son would be sent to his room for life and never again see the light of day and wither away, pale and disconsolate. But we tested the wind with our fingers and it didn't seem too bad, so we brought the board, which was five feet long and fatter than it should have been. We'd worked on that board every day during the summer with wax and affection and dreams of glory. The board was obstreperous, however, and no matter what we did, it was too much for just one of us to manage on his bike. So we decided to carry it between us, and in this ungainly manner we set off for the beach.

For a while all was well except for the amazed looks of passersby and their occasional ostensibly witty remarks. Why people try to be

witty when the only available audience is the very people they are trying unsuccessfully to be witty about is a mystery to me. Finally we
climbed the embankment up to the highway and headed south to the
beach. Just then my brother reminded me that we would have to pass
through the tollbooth constructed so that city planner Robert Moses
could recoup the tax dollars he had spent providing Jones Beach as a
gift to the people of New York State. Our older brother worked there
as a toll collector, but he wasn't the sort of brother you might casually
ask a favor of while he was on the job, and there was no way around
the toll unless you could swim with your bike on your back. We decided we would worry about this when we came to it.

We soon grew weary, and the surfboard was incredibly heavy, so
we stopped and ate a sandwich as the cars whizzed by, and one car
threw a beer can at us for no reason we could tell. Because we were
both reading the Hardy Boys books at that time and wanted to be de-
tectives, we got the license-plate number and my kid brother, who had
a ferocious memory, memorized it and also wrote it in the sand just
in case. We proceeded on. Now there were flies and mosquitoes but
also rabbits at the foot of the dense bushes beside the shoulder. We
came to the first bridge and after a brief discussion decided that we
would walk our bicycles one by one along the curb and then come
back for the surfboard. A guy slowed down to help us (or rob us)
as we were walking the surfboard over but we waved him on impatiently, using the glowering faces we admired on construction workers
and our older brother who worked at the tollbooth up ahead. We used
the same plan at the second bridge, although this time a gust of wind
did come up and we were almost blown into the highway just as a
truck roared past and we were nearly obliterated and we made a deep
and secret pact never ever to tell our parents about this incident, a
pact I am reluctant to break even now. This experience made us hungry, so we ate our other sandwiches and drank our sodas and buried
the cans in the sand for archaeologists to find in the twenty-seventh
century and proceeded on. The highway led inevitably to the tollbooth
and, as expected, there was no way around without being seen from
the state-police office; Robert Moses was no fool. As our mother said,

you had to admire the devious energy of the man, even though he was an arrogant tyrant who should be in prison for destroying a thousand neighborhoods and their vibrant cultural fabric.

By now we were exhausted and hot and thirsty and both of us would have cried if the other hadn't been there. We sat for a few moments reconnoitering and then my kid brother, to my amazement, walked right up to the tollbooth and knocked on our older brother's window and our older brother took a break and drove over in a battered gray state truck and put us and our bicycles and our surfboard in the truck and took us to West End 2, which was and probably still is the best beach in New York for surfing, and we surfed there for the rest of the afternoon, not very well, until the end of our older brother's shift, at which point he came to get us in his Ford Falcon and carried us home. On the way we were so tired that we both fell asleep together in the narrow back seat. We were so tired that we stayed asleep even after we got home and our older brother quietly unloaded our bicycles and the surfboard. I did wake groggily when he closed the trunk of the Falcon, and I saw him with one hand on each bicycle and the surfboard under his arm as he walked to the garage to put them away. Even today all these years later, when I think of our older brother, that's one of the first things I remember. You'd think I'd remember him in his tuxedo on the day he was married, or in his flowing academic robe on the day he earned his doctorate, or hoisting up his kids delightedly like tiny loaves of bread on the days that they were born, or even gaunt and grinning in the weeks before he died. But, no, it is him tall and thin and silent as he walked our bicycles and our surfboard back to the garage at dusk that I remember most—a slight thing by the measurement of the world, yet to me not slight at all but huge and crucial and holy.

VI.

I Walked Out So Full of
Hope I'm Sure I Spilled
Some by the Door

Chessay

My son asked me to play chess yesterday. It was Easter. When a child asks you to play chess you say yes. He is twenty years old and an excellent chess player. I taught him to play when he was five years old. He first beat me when he was thirteen years old. What I remember best from that day is his slow smile when he and I realized, a few moves before the end, that he had toppled the king. I remember too that he did not crow or caper or shout or cackle but instead reached across the board and shook my hand, as I had taught him to do, out of respect for the game, and for your opponent, in whose mind you have been swimming for an hour. Chess at its best is a deeply intimate game in which you can delve into another person's mind and if you are lucky you get a glance a hint an intimation of your opponent's character and creativity, the cast of his mind, the flare of her personality, how he confronts difficulties, how rash or calm she is, how willing to be surprised, how well he loses, how poorly she wins.

He came out along his left wing, immediately establishing his knights, immediately forcing me to scuffle and skitter around on defense. My queen roared off her throne snarling and forced her way all the way to his back line but he deftly boxed her in with yapping pawns. Sometimes I think the pawn is the most powerful piece of all. Revolutions and religions begin with ragged beggars from the wilderness. I sent my bishops slicing here and there. My pawns grappled and died. He missed one golden fatal chance with a knight. The knight's curious sidelong move is the deepest genius of chess; it is the one piece that does not move in linear fashion, the one piece with a geometry of its own, the piece that goes its own way.

In a moment he will be thirty. I want to stare at him across the board for a week. He catches me in a mistake that takes me forever to redress. I don't know how to say any words that would catch the way I love him. I want him to outwit me. I want to win and I want to lose and I want to savor how deftly I am defeated. I often wonder if I have been a good enough father. A good father teaches his son how to kill the king. He makes an infinitesimal mistake and my rooks close in grimly. I have prayed desperately to die before he does. I would like to teach his children to play chess. I would like to show them how, if you are lucky, you can see inside your opponent, only occasionally, only dimly, only for a few minutes, but for those few minutes you get a hint an intimation a glance at who lives inside the castle of his body. What we see of each other is only a bit of who we are. I want to invent new words for what we mean when we say the word *love*. *Chess* can be a wonderful word for that. *Chess* is a lovely word that can't be spoken. After the game we shake hands and I think never in the history of the world was there ever a man happier to be a father than me. Never in the whole long bristling history of the world.

Lines Hatched on the Back Porch
of Eudora Welty's House
in Jackson, Mississippi

Where Miss Welty sat too nearly every evening for seventy years
As the darkness descended like a dress, she said, and then a glass
Of bourbon with which to watch the evening news, grace and evil
Delivered right to the house, and ice from the narrow refrigerator
Where once a friend stored an owl, and then maybe some old jazz
Records, or a book from one of the teetering towers everywhere,
When I was a child I thought books were mere natural wonders
Coming up like grass, or maybe the last letter of the day hammered
On that ancient typewriter, she finally got an electric typewriter but
Noted tartly that *all it ever seemed to say was hurry up hurry up*
Or maybe just sitting late on the porch inhaling the pines and roses
And cedars and magnolias and last murmurs of the mockingbirds,
And thinking about her mom and dad and brother, all long gone,
Who gave her the cool room upstairs because she was the only girl
And here she is many years later, let's say a night when she's eighty
Wandering around *laying pages on the rug or the bed or the table*
To find the shape and bone of the story, its smell and its weight,
Finding out the thing that matters with a story of any kind at all,
Where is the voice coming from? And there have been so many
Braided voices in this house and this head. *Memory is a living thing,*
She thinks, rattling the ice in her glass just to interest the wary owls
Up in the redolent myrtles and pines. *As we remember we discover,*
And my memory is my dearest treasure. She thinks of the young
Interviewer who was here this morning from the college newspaper.

The girl who asked, what was it like to have led such a sheltered life?
And Miss Welty smiles and shivers her ice one last time and says aloud
To the mockingbirds and owls and reporters and readers and scholars
A sheltered life can be a daring life, as a daring life comes from within,
And steps inside and closes the door and, humming, heads to bed.

Joey's Doll's Other Arm

...might be in Denmark for all I know, or Delaware, or perhaps, as my daughter surmises, it disappeared, evanesced, disarmed itself one morning—gathered all its armish energy, curled itself into a fleshy fist, and punched out of this earthly plane. All I know is that one day it was attached to Joey's doll's starboard side and then the next day it wasn't. For a time it drifted around the house, looking eerily like a lost finger, and then it made its way out onto the lawn, where I saw a jay worrying it one morning (a Steller's jay, the size of a robin on steroids), and then it vanished.

My wife thinks the jay took it, and that the arm now hangs out of a nest nearby, not unlike the teenage arms hanging lazily out of one of the battered roaring cars that clatter and roar up my street, arms that come to life and extend fingers at me when I roar at them from my porch. My daughter thinks that one of the foxes from the nearby fir forest took it, and that the arm is now mounted over the foxy fireplace as a sort of trophy. Liam, who is Joey's twin brother, one minute younger, doesn't think about the arm, or at least he doesn't talk about it. But Joey thinks about it all the time.

He asks about it every morning, when I lift him out of his crib.

"Arm?" he asks, holding up the doll to show me its gaping armpit.

"I don't know where the dolly's arm is, Joey."

"Dolly arm owie."

"Damn right, Joey. Dolly sans extremity. Dolly a Democrat—no right wing."

"Owie."

"Yeah, owie. Maybe the arm is out on the grass. Want to look?"

And off goes my oldest son at a gallop toward the glassy front door in search of the grassy arm of his beloved. To no avail. But I admire his persistence, his condensed breath in a circle on the glass of the door every morning, the unflagging relentless drive of his love, and it is that ferocious affection of which I wish to speak this morning, only a few minutes after Joey galumphed out of the room, his sneakers hammering the beat of his desire on the old oak floor.

All my life I have thought about love, perhaps ever since I was Joey's age and learning then, as he is now, to say *I love you mama* (*Yaiyuffumama,* his voice a clear reedy silvery flute), and then through the thunderstorm of pubescent crushes and daydreams, and headlong into first serious loves, and then luckily, by the grace of whatever gods you wish to summon to this sentence, married love, which I understand less by the year and savor all the more. And then other rich, broad loves: my children, an island in the Atlantic, my dearest friends, woodland hawks, the flinty hipbone of the New England forest, the moist matted nap of the Northwest woods. And also, waxing and waning, delightful and puzzling, a love for God. Or god. Or our spiritual nature. Or whatever you want to call that occasional overpowering sense of a Sense under and through things.

Often I think we are afraid to speak frankly of God or gods because we cannot read that Mind, because so often religion is evil and greedy and bloody, because faith is so quixotic and unreasonable, because *spirituality* is a word as overloaded with connotation as a log truck top-heavy with the bones of trees. But because we sensibly fear a label does not mean we should be afraid of the content, and I wonder, on this bright morning, if divine love is not unlike Joey's doll's other arm: nearby, sensed, remembered, yearned for, searched for day after day after day, our breaths condensing on the glassy panes of this spectacularly inexplicable world as we look for it.

I also think that this lush, troubled world, so ferociously lovely, so plundered and raped and endangered, is itself a seething river of divine love, in much the same way as Joey is. Like Joey, the ship of this world came to me from seas unknown; both were made elsewhere and placed in my hands like squirming jewels, and my work and active prayer is to cherish them, to protect them, to try to hear in them Maker's music, to sing a little of that music myself. Love comes in so many guises, and a deep respect and affection for cedar trees or sockeye salmon is close cousin to a deep respect and affection for children and neighborhoods and wives. Love is a continuum; so a man who says he loves his wife and children is at the least blind and at the most evil if he votes to rape land (a very slow-moving creature) and kill creatures. He is in a real sense killing his own loved ones; he is killing himself.

The truest words I ever heard about divine love were uttered once by a friend as a grace before a meal. He bowed his head, in the guttering candlelight, steam rising from the food before him, the fingers of the cedar outside brushing the window, and said, "We are part of a Mystery we do not understand, and we are grateful."

Agreed. And now to join Joey in searching for it.

The Room in the Firehouse

So I went to a meeting with a friend. It was early in the morning in the town's firehouse. The firemen had lent a room to these meetings for thirty years. My friend was rattled and defensive. It was the first time my friend had been to such a meeting. We sat in a quiet corner. Most people sat against the walls but a few sat at a table in the center of the room. There were women and men of all ages. The young man next to me fidgeted the entire ninety minutes of the meeting except when it was his turn to speak. A woman across from us knitted furiously the whole meeting, stopping only when it was her turn to speak. People took turns speaking. There was no particular order. A slight man in a baseball cap spoke first. He was wry and funny about the hash he had made of his life. Most of the people who spoke were wry and funny. One man's voice shook when he spoke and the man next to him reached over and put his gnarled hand on his shoulder. Even though many of the speakers were wry and funny, their stories were not. Their stories were awful. Wives walking out the door with children, and police cars and police vans and police officers and court judges and probation officers, and broken teeth and bones, and having to camp in city parks, and companions who froze to death in alleys, and waking up in strange rooms with strange people, and your own children quietly locking the door when they saw it was you on the front porch, and security officers escorting you off the premises as you walked along with all the stuff that had been in your office cubicle now crammed into a big cardboard box, and walking out of meetings like this because meetings like this were for losers, not for you, and you didn't need this vaguely religious holding-hands stuff, and then sitting right by the door so you could leave when it got to be too much, but then later taking a seat all the way inside, and maybe someday you would even sit at the table, although sitting at the table means you have to be savagely honest with yourself and everyone else about what you cannot do without help, and being that kind of desperately honest is unbelievably awfully hard.

But I sat in a quiet corner of a firehouse and listened as one person after another *was* that searingly honest, and did speak openly and ruefully about what one man called the delicious disaster, and I was so moved I could not speak for some moments after the meeting ended. My friend did not seem moved and strode out of the meeting appearing glad that it was over, and dismissive of those poor people, and I wished my friend was not dismissive of those people. It seemed to me that those people were the wealthiest people I ever saw in honest humility. It seemed to me they were battling ferociously to turn horror into some small shivering peace and maybe even someday somehow a shy stagger of joy. It seemed to me that they were great because they knew they were not great, healthy because they knew they were ill, admirable because they knew they were not admirable at all by the measures of the real world, as another man called the world outside the room in the firehouse.

There was something great in that room. There is something great in all the thousands of rooms like it in America, the millions of rooms like it around the world. I don't have a good word for that great thing, but I saw it, staggering like a new foal, from where I sat silently in the corner. My friend did not yet appear to see it, or try to reach for it, and there was nothing I could do to make that happen. But perhaps part of the great thing that happens in these rooms is that, though no one can open that window for anyone else, everyone can applaud when someone does reach for that crack of light, shyly, shaking a little. My friend and I heard that applause several times in the room in the firehouse, and it sounded like the most wonderful painful music to me.

Selections from Letters
and Comments on My Writing

Why do you abuse punctuation so? What has punctuation ever done to you? Where were you educated, if you were educated? Did you not study grammar? Breaking all the rules of syntax, apparently deliberately, does not constitute art. The fur-trapper in your novel is an evil man and a liar and you should be ashamed of yourself. Why are there no dogs in your novel? Do you have something against dogs? How can a man write an entire novel about a town and not mention a single dog? In several of your essays you say that cats are the brooding spawn of Satan. Why do you say such things? Are you trying to be funny? I will assume that you are trying to be humorous but it certainly is not amusing to us in the cat community. In your book about a vineyard you refer constantly to your lovely research assistant. I just discovered from the Web that you are married, and have been married for many years. Does your wife know about your research assistant? In your book about a vineyard you veer off every other chapter into whatever seems to be in your head at that time. Why did your publisher let that happen? Our book club read this book and we got into such an argument about it being inane or brilliant that the book club was dissolved and now I have to find a new book club, for which I blame the author. In your novel about seafaring there is a mistake on page 211. In your novel about a pine marten there is a mistake on page 208. In your novel about the Oregon coast there may be a mistake on page one, second paragraph, but your writing style is so weird that it may not be a mistake. I find your ostensibly "spiritual" essays to be nothing more than religious claptrap deviously designed to sell the scurrilous agenda of the Papist Church. Your nominally "spiritual" essays should bear a large warning sticker on the cover warning sensible and reasonable readers to stay away. I have now read all three of the books that you claim are "poetry" but not one of them is anything near as good as everything Mary Oliver ever wrote. (To that reader I wrote back, agreeing wholeheartedly.) Why do you not use quotation marks in your novels? Our book club just read your novel and one of our members pointed out that there are no adverbs in the entire book. Did you do that on purpose or was that an accident? I have to write a paper about your writing and when I go to Wikipedia it says you were born in 1935 and 1956. How is that possible? Is that because you are Canadian? Our class is studying your essay about hummingbirds and we do not understand the ending. Do you? Our class read your book about hearts and when our teacher asked *What was he thinking?* we were all thinking exactly that. Our book club had to read your novel for our April meeting and my question to you is this: who were you trying to ape and copy, James Joyce or Jorge Luis Borges? Please respond to this question: I have ten dollars riding on Borges.

Billy Blake's Trial

A cold January day, Chichester, England. A "fitfully wet day" along the English coast, according to the *Sussex Weekly Advertiser*. Midmorning—a melancholy time, too early for lunch, too early for whiskey, breakfast a fond memory.

In the Chichester Guildhall a man named Youatt, a minister, strolls into a courtroom. He is a court recorder, charged with shorthand accounting of trial proceedings. The room in which he found himself was probably made almost entirely of wood: wooden benches, wooden railings, a wooden witness-box adjacent to the wooden magistrate's seat, wooden floor, sometimes a wooden judge. There were probably two oil paintings to either side of the magistrate's seat. One was almost certainly of the King—George III at the time. The other was usually of a national hero of some sort; let us say it is a portrait of the genius poet John Milton, a man who looked like a cart horse. Both paintings were probably enormous, as huge paintings were then considered dashing. No other ornaments are visible in the room, although there were almost certainly mountains of loose papers on the two counselors' tables.

Nothing happens to the Reverend Mister Youatt in his wooden room for a good long while. In a sense this stultifying pause is very English. Nothing happens for long stretches in England. It is the English way—white bread, thin tea, sex on Saturday. A land of hedgerows and gardens, amid which the people dream of order and porter. A slow land, a dreamy land. On this day, however, in about fifteen minutes, Mr. William Blake, age forty-seven, a resident of nearby

Felpham for three years, will be tried for sedition against George III, King of England, said treasonous acts being assault and battery on the person of Private John Scolfield of the Royal Dragoon Guards, and dragging the private down the street by his collar, and stuffing the private bodily into his barracks, and the vehement utterance of many seditious expressions, viz.: "Damn the King," "You Soldiers are all Slaves," and "If Bonaparte should come he would be master of Europe in an Hour's Time," etc., etc. The case, *Rex. v. Blake,* will be tried before a jury, six magistrates, and the Duke of Richmond. Counsel for the defense, Mr. Samuel Rose. First witness for the prosecution, Private John Cock of the Royal Dragoon Guards. Witnesses for the defense, various.

> Now is my grief at worst, incapable of being
> Surpassed; but every moment it accumulates more & more,
> It continues accumulating to eternity; the joys of God advance,
> But my griefs advance also, for ever & ever without end.
> O that I could cease to be! Despair! I am Despair,
> Created to be the great example of horror & agony; also my
> Prayer is vain. I called for compassion; compassion mock'd;
> Mercy & pity threw the gravestone over me, & with lead
> & iron bound it over me forever.

Blake was nervous about the trial, damned nervous. It had already cost him a hundred pounds simply for bail—money he had to borrow from friends—and the prospect of losing the case was terrifying. England had declared war on Napoleon in May, the country was an unruly bundle of nerves, and rumors of French invasion were rife along the southern coast. It was also rumored that Napoleon had assembled fleets of flatboats in every creek and harbor on the Channel; to fend off these invaders, troops of dragoons had been quartered in various coastal towns. Thus came Scolfield's troop to Felpham. Under these circumstances few accusations could be more serious than that of sedition, and the fact that Scolfield was a soldier boded ill.

Adding to the actual physical danger of Blake's position was its inconvenient timing. Blake and his wife, Catherine, had spent this last year in Felpham itching to leave. They were ready to move back to London in September when Scolfield filed charges in August. Felpham, which Blake had hoped would be "a sweet place for Study," had been a bust: Catherine was constantly sick, his neighbor William Hayley badgered him incessantly, and the weather was unrelentingly, angrily, eternally gray. London, which he had fled cursing its filth and meanness, now looked delicious. "I can carry on my visionary studies in London unannoy'd," he wrote to his London friend Thomas Butts. "There I can converse with my friends in Eternity, See Visions, Dream Dreams & prophecy & speak Parables unobserv'd & at liberty from the Doubts of other Mortals. I assure you that, if I could have return'd to London a Month after my arrival here, I should have done so, but I was commanded by my Spiritual friends to bear all, to be silent, & to go through all without murmuring."

> What is the price of Experience? do men buy it for a song?
> Or wisdom for a dance in the street? No, it is bought with the price
> Of all that a man hath, his house, his wife, his children.
> Wisdom is sold in the desolate market where none come to buy,
> & in the wither'd field where the farmer plows for bread in vain.

In Felpham, Blake had hired a man named William to tend to his garden. The man was an ostler, or horse groom, at the nearby Fox Inn. On the morning of August 12, Blake emerged from his cottage to find two men in his garden. One was William; the other was Private Scolfield, who, unbeknownst to Blake, had been invited into the garden by the gardener.

"I desired [Scolfield], as politely as was possible, to go out of the Garden," Blake explained in a letter to Butts. "He made me an impertinent answer. I insisted on his leaving the garden; he refused. I still persisted in desiring his departure; he then threaten'd to knock out my Eyes, with many abominable imprecations & with some contempt for my Person; it affronted my foolish pride. I therefore took him by the Elbows & pushed him before me until I had got him out; there I had intended to have left him, but he, turning about, put himself into a Posture of Defiance, threatening & swearing at me. I, perhaps foolishly & perhaps not, stepped out at the Gate, &, putting aside his blows, took him again by the Elbows, &, keeping his back to me, pushed him forward down the road about fifty yards—he all the while endeavouring to turn round & strike me, & raging & cursing, which drew out several neighbours; at length, when I had got him to where he was Quarter'd, which was very quickly done, we were met at the Gate by the Master of The Fox Inn (who is the proprietor of my Cottage), & his wife & Daughter & the Man's Comrade & several other people. My Landlord compell'd the Soldiers to go indoors, after many abusive threats against me & my wife from the two soldiers: but not one word of threat on account of Sedition was utter'd at that time."

& then the Knave begins to snarl.
& the Hypocrite to howl:
& all his good Friends shew their private ends,
& the Eagle is known from the Owl.

Three days later Private Scolfield swore out a formal complaint of sedition by the "Miniature Painter" William Blake against the King. Scolfield's account had Blake delivering a lengthy and bloodthirsty speech during which he shouted that he would cut the throats of his fellow Englishmen at Bonaparte's command, among other savageries. Scolfield also swore that Mrs. Blake issued forth from the cottage like a Fury and shouted that "altho' she was but a Woman, she would fight for Bonaparte as long as she had a drop of blood in her." Scolfield's account ends with Mrs. Blake telling her "said Husband" to eject the soldier, with Blake seizing the peaceful Scolfield by the collar, and with Blake damning the King as loudly at the top of his voice.

Cold snows drifted around him:
Ice cover'd his loins around.

The matter went to a grand jury in October 1803 at the Michaelmas Quarter Sessions in nearby Petworth. Blake attended, accompanied by his gardener. To Blake's dismay, the jury found Scolfield's charges of sedition and assault worthy of trial—the "bills were true," in the phrase of the day—which meant that he would be formally tried before a judge and jury in January. It was Blake's right, as defendant, to provide the court with his account of the matter, if he so chose, and to list points of evidence that he or his lawyer would muster in his defense. Blake did so, in a businesslike memorandum titled "In Refutation of the Information and Complaint of John Scolfield, a private Soldier, Etc." The memo ends with this editorial flourish:

"If such Perjury as this can take effect, any Villain in [the] future may come & drag me & my Wife out of our House, & beat us in the Garden or use us as he please or is able, & afterwards go & swear our Lives away. Is it not in the Power of any Thief who enters a Man's Dwelling & robs him, or misuses his Wife or Children, to go & swear as this Man has sworn?"

> Los seized his Hammer & Tongs; he laboured at his resolute Anvil
> Among indefinite Druid rocks & snows of doubt & reasoning.
> Enraged & stifled without & within,
>   in terror & woe, he threw his
> Right Arm to the north, his left Arm to the south, & his Feet
> Stamped the nether Abyss in trembling & howling & dismay.

Enter, with a hacking cough, Mr. Samuel Rose. He is a thin and sickly man about thirty years old, a friend of both Hayley and of the poet William Cowper. Hayley, who has already shelled out most of Blake's bail, hires Rose to defend Blake at Chichester Sessions.

The prosecution argued first, as is the custom to this day in English (and American) law, and after statement of the charge by Private Scolfield and corroborating testimony by Private Cock, Scolfield's lawyer hammered away at the "atrocity and malignity" of the charge, figuring that if the jury could be awed by the seditious imprecations that had supposedly issued from Blake's mouth, they would ignore the fact that the only eyewitness, the ostler, was prepared to swear that Blake said nothing of the kind. This tactic, called prosecuting the crime, sometimes works with serious charges, since juries are anxious to assign blame for such crimes; the more serious the offense, the more likely they are to convict someone.

Counselor Rose tooled his defense accordingly. His speech, "taken in short Hand by the Revd. Mr. Youatt," opens with complete agreement that such an offense is atrocious and malignant beyond words: "If there be a man who can be found guilty of such a transgression, he must apply to some other person to defend him," says Rose, icily. "I certainly think that such an offence is incapable of extenuation. My task is to shew that my client is not guilty of the words imputed to him, not to shew that [such words] are capable of any mitigated sense."

Having distanced himself and his client from the devilry of the charge, Rose methodically sets out the pieces of his argument like chessmen. One, Blake has been a loyal subject of the King all his forty-seven years. Two, Blake is a friend of local hero and noted patriot Hayley, who would never have allowed a rebel into his house. Three, Blake is an artist, and therefore apolitical. ("His art has a tendency, like all the other fine arts, to soften every asperity of feeling & of character, & to secure the bosom from the influence of those tumultuous & discordant passions, which destroy the happiness of mankind.") Four, Scolfield is an undependable witness—he has been broken from sergeant to private on account of drunkenness. Five, the charge prima facie doesn't make sense—is Blake, a sensitive artist, likely to storm from his house to utter "malignant & unintelligible discourse to those who are most likely to injure him for it"? Six, the ostler, who saw and heard the whole row, denies the charge wholly. Seven, the testimony of Private Cock, who stated that he emerged from his barracks to hear Blake damning King, country, and soldiers, is contradicted by a woman named Mrs. Grinder, who was next to Cock by the door of the barracks, and who says the poet said nothing of the kind.

"I will call my witnesses [the ostler and Mrs. Grinder] & you shall hear their account," sums up Rose. "You will then agree with me that they totally overthrow the testimony of these Soldiers...."

At this point, shockingly, Rose collapsed, overcome with the tension and with the effects of a nervous disease that would kill him a few months later. The court was in an uproar for several minutes.

> Lightnings of discontent broke on all sides round
> & murmurs of thunder rolling heavy long & loud over the mountains

Rose was helped to his feet but could not carry on, and because there was suddenly no defense lawyer, the defense witnesses were not called. The chairman of the Bench of Magistrates, the Duke of Richmond (who, according to Hayley, disliked Blake intensely and was for political reasons itching to convict him), sent the jury off to its deliberations, and the packed house settled back to wait for a verdict.

It could not have been much later than two o'clock p.m. when the jury retired; the trial had begun at ten a.m., only the two soldiers had testified, and there had been only one full-length summation, the prosecution's. If we generously allow half an hour for Rose's suddenly aborted speech (it is 1,650 words in Youatt's account), and guess that there was a lunch break, or an adjournment of some kind, or that Blake's repeated shouting of "False!" during Scolfield's testimony (a boy at the trial later told the journalist Alexander Gilchrist that what he remembered best from that day was Blake's "flashing eye") held up matters, or that attending to the fallen Rose may have taken a while, we may have pushed the clock to three o'clock or so. But the jury did not return its verdict until nearly eight o'clock p.m.

So Blake sat there in the courtroom at the Guildhall, on a dank day, his lawyer silenced, his wife sick at home, his freedom and future in the hands of people he did not know, in a county he had been itching to leave for years, for five hours.

> How long will ye vex my soul,
> & break me in pieces with words?

If this essay was a movie there would be a natural break at this point; the camera would pan around Blake sitting there at the table, eyes flashing, the murmuring crowd staring at him, the Duke of Richmond glaring from the bench, Scolfield glaring from the prosecution's table, Rose wheezing in a corner, Hayley up in the balcony signing autographs, the Reverend Mr. Youatt leaning back in his chair exhausted. Perhaps the camera would zoom in on Blake's round face ("he had a broad pale face and a large full eye," wrote the memoirist Crabb Robinson), always keying on his eyes, using the ferocious glare in them as an anchor for the frame. His eyes were gray and slightly protuberant, an effect heightened by his receding hairline. He had a firm chin, a considerable nose, and the look of a furious hawk when he was angry. The camera sidles up to Blake's face, the hubbub in the room gets a little louder, Blake turns slightly to stare right into the camera, his glaring eye FILLING THE FRAME. . . .

Which does a fade-and-flip so fast it barely registers on the viewer, and now the camera is retreating from the same ferocious eye but the eye is in the face of four-year-old Billy Blake, second son of James Blake, hosier and haberdasher, and we are into the flashback scene, which will cover, in a series of cross-cut jumps, the forty-three years between 1761, when Blake, age four, saw God, "who put His head in the window and set him a-screaming," according to his wife, and 1804, when Blake is the quiet eye of a swirling hubbub in Chichester's Guildhall.

> And then I think of Blake, in the dirt and sweat of London—a boy
> staring through the window, when God came
> fluttering up.
> Of course, he screamed,
> seeing the bobbin of God's blue body
> leaning on the sill,
> and the thousand-faceted eyes.
>
> —Mary Oliver, "Spring Azures"

At age eight Blake reported to his mother that he had seen the prophet Ezekiel under a tree. His mother beat him. At age ten he reported that he had seen a tree filled with angels, their "bright angelic wings bespangling every bough like stars." His father beat him. A month later, as he stood at the edge of a field watching haymakers at work, he saw angels walking toward him through the rye. His parents stopped beating him and sent him to art school, a decision made easier by the fact that the boy was a "booby" who spent all his time in his father's haberdashery drawing on the backs of bills. At age fourteen he became an engraver; at age twenty-four he married a slim dark-eyed girl named Catherine, who calmed him by cupping his feet in her hands when he shook with visions.

For the next twenty-three years Blake drew, painted, engraved, printed, colored, stippled, and lithographed. He opened a print shop, which immediately went bust. He invented a new form of engraving after he had a dream in which his dead brother Robert explained it to him. He wrote songs and then simple poems and then vast books of complex poems, many of which he engraved and printed himself, in books that he and Catherine painted and bound by hand. They lived on Green Street, Broad Street, Poland Street, the Hercules Buildings, in Felpham, on South Molton Street, and in the Strand. He sometimes made money and sometimes did not. Mostly he did not. To earn a living he did engravings on commission and drawings and watercolors for books and magazines; meanwhile, at night, at dawn, and often when he was supposed to be working on commissions, he wrote his huge poems and engraved them onto copper plates and printed them and watercolored the sheets and bound them into books, which he offered for sale at outrageous prices.

Here are the names of some of his books: *The Marriage of Heaven and Hell*; *The Book of Los*; *The Everlasting Gospel*; *The Book of Thel*; *The Book of Urizen*; *The Song of Los*; *The Four Zoas*; *Songs of Innocence and of Experience shewing the Two Contrary States of the Human Soul*; *Milton*; and *Jerusalem*. These last two were among his last, and both were begun at Felpham, before the trial. It is quite possible that Blake was writing *Milton* on the morning of August 12, when he walked out into his garden and noticed Private John Scolfield, of His Majesty's Royal Dragoons, standing at the garden gate, with a sneer upon his face.

> If you account it Wisdom when you are angry to be
>   silent and
> Not to shew it, I do not account that Wisdom, but Folly.
> Every Man's Wisdom is peculiar to his own Individuality.

Between three o'clock, when the jury retired, and eight o'clock, when the foreman stood to announce the verdict, Blake probably remained seated. Possibly he read, drew, or painted. He apparently had an astonishing capacity for concentration, and many times he spent eight hours at a time writing or drawing. It may be in this case that he simply sat there in the room thinking. There were no rules then, as there are none now, about activity during intermissions in trials; while the jury is deliberating, the accused, if he or she is not physically restrained, may stand on his head, imitate a cricket, mutter poems, or stare abstractedly into space. But this interregnum ends at the moment that the jury files back into the courtroom and the foreman stands and William Blake stands and stretches himself to his full height (about 5 feet 5 inches), and waits to hear whether he is a free man or whether he will be deported to Australia or hung by the neck until he is dead.

> Every Night and every Morn
> Some to Misery are Born.
> Every Morn and every Night
> Some are Born to sweet delight.
> Some are Born to sweet delight,
> Some are Born to Endless Night.

The courtroom hushes; Blake's eyes are nearly popping out of his head as the foreman forms the words
Not
and then with a rush as the crowd begins to roar

Guilty

and the courtroom explodes.

"In defiance of all decency," the Sussex *Weekly Advertiser* reported, the court was "thrown into an uproar by noisy exultations" and Blake was rushed out of the Guildhall in a roaring tide of townspeople. Hayley, ecstatic at the verdict, paused to drip some sarcasm on the judge, who he thought "bitterly prejudiced" against Blake: "I congratulate your Grace," said Hayley, "that after having been wearied by the condemnation of sorry Vagrants, you have at last had the gratification of seeing an honest man honorably delivered from an infamous persecution. Mr. Blake is a pacific, industrious, & deserving artist."

"I Know nothing of Him," snapped the Duke.

"True, my Lord, your Grace can know Nothing of Him," said Hayley, driving home the lance; "& I have therefore given you this Information: I wish your Grace a good Night." And off he went with Blake to dinner at the home of a mutual friend, Mrs. Poole.

I think about that dinner once in a while—what they ate, what Blake thought, who got drunk. Probably Hayley pontificated, as he did that well, and he had, after all, paid Blake's legal fees. I suppose Mrs. Poole smiled happily on her friend Blake, released from the shadow of the noose. And Billy Blake, Billy Blake—did he drink too much? Was he merry? Or did he sit there like a rock in a stream and think about his darling Kate, sick in bed in their new flat in London, and in his mind take her in his arms and tell her Kate, we are free, free, free, Kate, free, and the world will never again bind us and we will forge ahead and make our art and start over and earn our bread and worship the Lord and be free free free free free?

A Robin Red breast in a Cage
Puts all Heaven in a Rage.
A dove house fill'd with doves & Pigeons
Shudders Hell through all its regions.

William Blake, poet and printer, disappears almost completely from the public record after his trial. From 1804 through 1809 he scrambled without much success to make a decent living as an engraver. In 1809 he held a one-man show of his paintings at his brother's house. The show failed miserably, and its only reviewer, Robert Hunt of *The Examiner* magazine, called Blake "an unfortunate lunatic." In 1812 he exhibited four paintings at the Water Colour Society. In 1816 he was listed in *A Biographical Dictionary of the Living Authours of Great Britain and Ireland*, although the entry made him out to be an eccentric. From 1808 to 1819, Blake sold perhaps a couple of dozen engravings per year. He told an art dealer that he and Catherine made do for many years on an income of about a guinea a week; the equivalent, today, of a couple living for seven days on about twenty dollars. He kept working, though—"I never Stop," he told one friend—and the years slipped by until it was 1827 and he was suddenly seventy years old, "being only bones & sinews, All strings & bobbins like a Weaver's Loom."

> Trembling I sit day & night, my friends are
>   astonished at me,
> Yet they forgive my wanderings. I rest not
>   from my great task!

I have been writing this essay for more than a year now. I have been taking notes for it for five years. Over the course of those years I have asked myself, many times, why I'm doing this. A careful account of the trial for sedition of the poet and printer William Blake, in the year 1804, on a fitfully wet day in January, in a wooden room by the sea—why?

Answering this question is like trying to answer the very good question, Why do you write? I don't know why I write, exactly. Catharsis, the itch to make something shapely and permanent, the attempt to stare God in the eye, the attempt to connect deeply to other men and women, because I can't help myself, because there is something elevating in art, because I feel myself at my best when I am writing well. Because because because. Because this essay is my way of befriending and comprehending Billy Blake, whom I greatly admire in absentia.

Why do you admire him so?

Because he told the truth, because he shoved an insolent leering soldier down the road and stuffed him through a doorway, because he saw angels and saints and talked openly about his visions. Because he published his work himself. Because he was a tender and difficult and solicitous friend. Because he took great pride in his engraving and worked endlessly on plates to make them perfect. Because when he knew he was going to die he lay in his bed singing softly. Because he smiled at the deft poetry of the message when his wife served him an empty plate at dinner to remind him that they were starving. Because he wasn't satisfied with extant mythology and so built a vast grand impenetrable one of his own. Because in all the things he wrote he never mentioned his weight, which was ample, or his height, which was not. Because he single-handedly rescued the ampersand—&—from oblivion. Because in the few drawings of him he is alert, intent, attentive. Because even when his work was dictated whole to him by angels and prophets, he edited heavily. Because he and his wife used to sit naked in their garden and recite passages from *Paradise Lost*. Because when he was asked to recite his poems at parties he got up and removed his coat and sang his lyrics aloud while dancing around the room, which is why he was subsequently not invited to parties anymore. Because he taught his wife, a farmer's daughter, to read. Because he rose first every morning and laid the fire and made tea for her. Because he was endlessly exuberant. Because once at a dinner party he suddenly said to the child next to him, "May God make this world as beautiful to you as it has been to me," a sentence she remembered the rest of her life. Because he held his opinions firmly. Because his wife said she never saw his hands still unless he was asleep. Because to walk with him "was like walking on air and talking with the Prophet Isaiah," said his young friend George Richmond. Because he took great care to leave no debt at his death. Because he wrote and then threw away "six or seven epic poems as long as Homer, and twenty tragedies as long as Macbeth," judging them not worthy of publication or engraving. Because in the ringing fury of his lines there is also great mercy. Because even when he was sick unto death he engraved a little business card for his old friend George Cumberland. Because he could not stop painting and died with his pencil in his hand. Because he bought a new pencil two days before he died. Because the very last thing he drew was his wife's face.

It is this last detail that catches my heart.

But thou O Lord
Do with me as thou wilt!
for I am nothing,
& vanity.

I have scoured many books for accounts of Blake's last day. I'm not sure why. We all die in the end, and the grace or gracelessness with which we leave is meat only for the morbid. Yet I want to know how Billy stepped into the next room. I want to know how firmly he held his opinions in the face of annihilation. I want to know him in the last moments that he wore a body like mine, in the last moments that he saw crows, spoons, apples, angels. I want to hear his heart.

He died on a Sunday in late summer. By this time he was completely bedridden, "his ankles frightfully swelled, his chest disordered, old age striding on," noted a friend. Blake himself knew that he had not long to live. "Dear Cumberland," he had scribbled in April, "I have been very near the Gates of Death & have returned very weak & an Old Man feeble & tottering, but not in Spirit & Life, not in The Real Man, The Imagination, which Liveth for Ever. In that I am stronger & stronger as this Foolish Body decays...."

On the morning of August 12—exactly twenty-three years, to the day, after he met Private John Scolfield, of His Majesty's Royal Dragoons—Blake awoke early and painted for a couple of hours. Then, according to his wife, he said "I have done all I can" and dropped the painting on the floor. She sat down at his bedside.

"Kate, stay as you are. You have been an angel to me, I will draw you," he said.

When the drawing was finished he signed it "Mrs. Blake drawn by Blake," and wrote her name in large letters under his signature.

Then he began to sing.

He sang "Hallelujahs & songs of joy and triumph, with true ecstatic energy," for the rest of the afternoon—hymns and then, for hours, his own poems. At about six o'clock, he told Catherine that he was going to that country that all his life he had wished to see, and that he would always be about her.

"Then," wrote his friend Richmond (no relation to the Duke), who was at his bedside, "his Countenance became fair, His eyes Brighten'd, & He burst out Singing of the things he saw in Heaven," and he died.

> Have pity upon me, have pity upon me,
> O ye my friends;
> For the hand of God hath touched me.

After a minute Richmond reached over and closed his eyes—"to keep the visions in." Richmond then left. As he paused in the door, he looked back. The last thing he saw, he wrote later, was Catherine kissing William's hands.

Catherine died four years later. She often talked to her husband as if he was in the room, and in her last hours called continually to him, to say she was coming and would not be long from his side.

It is said that she died with one of his pencils in her hand.

On All Souls Day

All my life, when I thought about death coming for me,
I wondered *how* he would come, and what costumes he
Would wear (cancer coat? stroke suits?), and if I would
Be a weenie, whining all the way to the end, or die wry,
Smiling a bit and offering dry and entertaining remarks,
But now I think I know myself well enough to know I'll
Be seriously *interested* in the whole thing. Can you chat
with death, is that possible? Can you, you know, natter?
I am not kidding. Every death is a whole new way to die.
My stroke will be unlike Robert Louis Stevenson's—not
Just because he was younger or in Samoa or a lot thinner,
But because I am made of love and song and amusement
In ways he was not and could not know. My death is a new
Country not just for me but for my death. I feel a passing
Empathy for my death—it gets only the one shot at doing
What it is designed to do. We are weirdly sort of partners.
The poor bedraggled thing, waiting all these dozing years!
I suppose I used to wonder if you could dicker and outwit
Your death, but now only hope I will have a chance to dig
It, you know what I mean? I don't mean this in a macabre
Way. It's more like your death is a part of your life, right?
I don't want to live companionably with it for a long time,
But it *will* be absorbing to get to know it a little before we
Wander off into the wilderness. As soon as I die my death
Does too, but who knows what happens to who *I* was? It's

Like this: I might get a whole new gig, as an otter or a bee,
Or a glowering angel assigned to protect a Uruguayan boy,
But old death expires like a yellowed coupon you discover
In a coat you last wore to church to pray, on All Souls Day.

Two Anesthesiologists

I had occasion recently to spend half an hour listening to two anesthesiologists, which was unnerving, because I was supine and scared and about to endure their subtle craft, but fascinating, too, because they were seasoned and chatty and patently delighted to be quizzed about their work. I asked them all sorts of things, about their training and interests and nativities and hobbies and children and favorite music and writers; one of the two men, interestingly, was totally into old Roman writers such as Suetonius and Tacitus and Quintus Curtius Rufus, and he was startled and pleased when I told him I loved Plutarch and Edward Gibbon, and annually dipped back into both, to swim happily in Gibbon's endless sentences and in Plutarch's unreal ability to sketch a man's character in a brief anecdote. But what really got them going, so much so that we were all nearly late for the matter at hand, was my question about what last remarks patients mumbled as the anesthetics took hold. It seemed to me that perhaps those remarks would reveal something revelatory of the patients' priorities and state of mind, and this turned out to be true. They told me that they'd noticed gender differences, for example that men would often joke until the very second that they fell unconscious, probably as a defense against fear, while women were often very concerned about being properly covered with the blankets until the last possible second. In my experience, said one anesthesiologist, children tend not to cry or whimper, but to just stare at me in abject terror and fearful trust. A child on the table always rattles me. Always.

Many men and women, said the other anesthesiologist, murmur

something at the end about how if they do not emerge from the operation safely, could we please tell their loved ones how much they were loved? Please? And we always say yes we will, and we would, too, if it ever came to that, which it doesn't. We are good at what we do, very careful indeed, very attentive, ferociously attentive, you might say. But then, he said, starting to laugh, yes, there are some hilarious and really odd things that people murmur at the very end. One man whom I thought was out cold suddenly opened his eyes and said *Tell her the blue colander is under the sink.* Another guy said, in the very last second, *I didn't do it, I tell you I didn't.* One woman said, so quietly that I could barely make it out, *Why? Why? Just tell me why.* But you can easily read too much into it, said the other anesthesiologist. I mean, the vast majority of what people say as they fade out is stuff like *Can you scratch my foot?* and *Can I have another pillow?* and *Where are my car keys?,* that sort of thing. But sometimes they will say things that make you realize we are all little kids when it comes to surgery. Believe me, even doctors and nurses and anesthesiologists are little kids when they are on the table. I have heard people whisper to their moms, and ask Jesus to hold their hands, and ask me to hold their hands, and ask me to place photographs of their kids over their hearts during the procedure, which we cannot do, though I totally understand why you'd want your kids' faces over your heart if you were afraid you were fading out of the world forever.

We talked about how they'd handled being anesthetized themselves during small surgical procedures, and about how each and every patient was slightly different in the amount and type of anesthetic necessary, which is amazing when you think about it, how we can be so similar as regards anatomy and physiology but so individual at the same time. And then it was time for them to get to work on me, which they did. And I asked them afterward what, if anything, I had said at the very end, as I was fading out, and they grinned and said you were one of the ones who mumbled about your wife and kids, but you didn't ask us to put their photographs on your chest.

Joey

A while ago I got sick.
It was a thorough and major sick.
Lost use of the old hands and feet,
Which was, as you can imagine, weird.
My kids called the sickness The Thing.
The Thing went on for months and months.
I could tell you lots of stories about The Thing,
But there's only one story that I want to tell you:
Every morning my son got up early to help me
Put my socks on. I would sit on the back stairs
In the dark and he would wrestle my socks on
And neither of us would say any words and I
Still can't think of anything cooler than that.
I have racked my brains and considered
All the possibilities of love and I still
Return to that boy and those socks.
No matter what happens to me,
That happened to me.

A Prayer for You and Yours

Well, my first prayers as a parent were *before* I was a parent, because my slight extraordinary mysterious wife and I had been told by a doctor, bluntly and directly and inarguably, that we would not be graced by children, and I remember us walking out of the doctor's office, silently, hand in hand, and then opening the passenger door to our car for my wife, as my mother had taught all her sons to do or else she, my mom, would reach up and slap you gently on the back of the head for being a boor, and I helped my wife into the car, and bent down to escort the hem of her blue raincoat into the car before closing the door gently, and then I started to walk around to the driver's side, and I burst into tears, and bent over the trunk of the car, and sobbed for a moment.

My first prayers as a parent, those tears.

Then we prayed for a long time in all sorts of ways. I prayed in churches and chapels and groves and copses and hilltops and on the rocky beaches of the island where we lived at that time. I would have prayed to all the gods who ever were or ever would be except I know somehow deep in my heart that there is one Breath, one Imagination, one Coherent Mercy, as a friend of mine says, and that everything that is came from and returns to That which we cannot explain or understand, but can only try to perceive the spoor, clues, evidence, effect, the music in and through and under all things.

I have never thought that prayers of request can be answered; I do not think that is the way of the Mercy; yet we do whisper prayers of supplication; I think we always have, since long before our species arrived in this form. Sometimes I think that beings have been praying since there were such things as beings; I suspect all beings of every sort do pause and revere occasionally, and even if we think, with our poor piddly perceptive apparatus, that they are merely reaching for the sun, or drying their wings, or meditating in the subway station between trains, or chalking the lines of a baseball field ever so slowly and meticulously, perhaps they are praying in their own peculiar particular ways; who is to say? Who can define that which is a private message to an Inexplicable Recipient? So that he who says a scrawny plane tree straining for light in a city alley is not a prayer does not know what he is saying, and his words are wind and dust.

Three children were granted to us, a girl and then, together, one minute apart, two boys; and my prayers doubled, for now I knew fear for them, that they would sicken and die, that they would be torn by dogs and smashed by cars; and I felt even then the shiver of faint trepidation that someday, if they grew up safely, and did not suffer terrible diseases, and they achieved adulthood, that they would be heart-hammered by all sorts of things against which I could not protect or preserve them; and so I did, I admit it, sometimes beg the Coherent Mercy, late at night, for small pains as their lot, for relatively minor disappointments, for love affairs that would break apart but not savagely, for work that they would like and even maybe love. In the end, I remember vividly, I boiled all my prayers as a parent down to this one: Take me instead of them. Load me up instead of them. Let me eat the pains they were served for their tables. I don't think I ever fully understood the deep almost inexplicable love of the Christ for us, why he would accept his own early tortured death as a sacrifice, until I had been a father for a while.

Somehow being a father also slowly but surely changed the target of my prayers over the years; before we were granted children, I chatted easily and often with my man Yesuah ben Joseph, a skinny gnomic guy like me, a guy with a motley crew of funny brave hardworking boneheaded friends, a guy who liked to wander around outdoors, a guy who delighted in making remarks that were puzzling and memorable and riddlish, a guy—I felt like I knew him pretty well, what with us both being guys and all, and I had confided stuff to him not only as a child, but again after the years during which every Catholic boy in my experience ran screaming and shouting away from the Church, away from authority and power and corporate corruption and smug arrogant pompous nominal bosses issuing proclamations and denouncing dissent.

You tiptoe back toward religion, in my experience, cautiously and nervously and more than a little suspicious, quietly hoping that it wasn't all smoke and nonsense, that there is some deep wriggle of genius and poetry and power and wild miracle in it, that it is a language you can use to speak about that for which we have no words; and in my case, as in many others I know, this was so, and I saw for the first time in my life that there were two Catholic Churches, one a noun and the other a verb, one a corporation and the other a wild idea held in the hearts of millions of people who are utterly uninterested in authority and power and rules and regulations, and very interested indeed in finding ways to walk through the bruises of life with grace and humility.

So when I tiptoed back into Catholicism, and began taking it seriously, and began exploring and poking under the corporate hood, curious and fascinated by the revolutionary genius under the Official Parts, it was because I was a father, and knew that I needed a language with which to speak to my children of holiness and prayer and miracle and witness and hope and faith; and I found, month by month as my children grew from squirming lumps to toddlers and willowy young people and now almost men and woman, that it was to Mary that I turned, both in desperation and in cheerful silent moments when I chanted the Hail Mary to myself while waiting for the coffee to boil.

Why? Because, I think, she was a mother—*is* a mother. He came out of her. That was a miracle. It is a miracle when a child emerges from his or her mother. I had seen this miracle not once but twice, with my own eyes, from very close to the field of action, and I think something awoke in me after that, something that knew she was there, available, approachable, patient, piercing. Not once in the days since my children were born have I ever felt her absence. I do not say this in a metaphorical way, or as a cool literary device, or as a symbolic hint. I mean what I said. I feel her near us. I have no opinion about visitations, other than to grin at the ones where people see her face in tortillas and on stop signs, and to wonder quietly about ones like that which occurred to Juan Diego on the Hill of Tepeyac, long ago, that poor man who had to return to the hill for proof to offer the ecclesiastic authority, who gaped when a shower of roses fell to the shivering floor. Perhaps most reports are hallucinations; perhaps all of them. But perhaps hallucinations are illuminations, and there are countless more things possible than we could ever dream. One thing I know at this age: if you think you know the boundaries and limits and extents of reality, you are a fool. Thus we pray.

I still pray for my children every day. So does my wife, in the morning, by the bed, on her knees, in her pajamas, with her face pressed down upon the blanket of the bed, abashed before the light of the Lord. I have seen this, though I try to be out of the bedroom so that she can pray in private; and every time I see it I get the happy willies, that she believes with such force and humility. But I pray on my feet, by the coffee pot, while walking, while waiting for eyeglasses, while stirring the risotto, while washing the dishes, while brushing my teeth, while scratching the dog. I pray that they would be happy. I pray that they will find work that is play. I pray that their hearts will not be stomped on overmuch—enough to form resilience, but not enough to crush their spirits. I pray that they will live long and be blessed by married love and be graced by children and maybe even grandchildren. I pray that their minds hum and sing and do not stutter and fail. I pray that they will not be savaged by illnesses, but be allowed to live healthy and happy for years beyond my ken and my own life. I still pray to die before they do. I still say thank you, every day, every single day, for being granted children at all; for I am a man who was told, bluntly and directly and inarguably, that my extraordinary bride and I would not be graced by children, and we walked out of the doctor's office, silently, hand in hand, and we wept.

Our first tears as parents.

We have cried many tears since, for many reasons, and our children have been tumultuous, and troubled, and in great danger, and our marriage has been wonderfully confusing, and troubled, and in great danger; but even now, all these years later, every few weeks, I will find myself in tears for what seems like no reason at all; and I know it is because we were blessed with children, three of them, three long wild prayers; and they are the greatest gifts a profligate Mercy ever granted shuffling muddled me. When I am in my last hour, when I am very near death, when I am so soon to change form and travel in unaccountable ways and places, I hope I will be of sound enough mind to murmur this, to our three children, and perhaps, if the Mercy has been especially ridiculously generous, our grandchildren: it was for you that I was here, and for you I prayed every day of your life, and for you I will pray in whatever form I am next to take. Lift the rock and I am there; cleave the wood and I am there; call for me and I will listen, for I hope to be a prayer for you and yours long after I am dust and ash. Amen.

His Listening[*]

A mong the many things that my father was very good at was this: when you said something to him, anything at all, anything in the range from surpassingly subtle to stunningly stupid, he would listen carefully and attentively and silently, without interrupting, without waiting with increasing impatience for you to finish so he could correct or top or razz you, and he would even wait a few beats after you finished your remarks, on the off chance that you had something else you wanted to add, and then he would ponder what you had said, and then, without fail, he would say something encouraging first, before he got around to commenting on what it was you said with such breathtaking subtlety or stupidity.

And he did this not once but many thousands of times, not just with me but also with my sister and brothers, and his lovely bride, our mother, and daughters-in-law and grandchildren and colleagues and friends, so that the number of times he listened patiently and attentively and scrupulously, and then politely waited a few beats to give a speaker a chance to dig deeper into or clamber hurriedly out of the hole he had just dug himself, and then said something gentle and encouraging before tacking finally toward the subject at hand, surely was a million or more, especially given the fact that he and our mother had many children together, and we are American Irish Catholics, which is to say

---

_{* This is the very last of the 173 consecutive "Epiphanies" columns that BD published in *The American Scholar,* "the longest tenure of any blogger by far," the editors noted, "and we hope his columns have enchanted, delighted, and enriched you as much as they have us."}

people soaked in three garrulous cultures, each one entranced by story and legend and myth and the tallest of tales.

I well remember some of my own remarkably ill-considered remarks to him, as a surly teenager, as a headlong young man, and as a formerly cocky middle-aged man, and in every one of those cases he was wonderfully consistent in his patience, his calm, his gentleness, his genuine absorption in what I was saying, even though what I was saying was sometimes the most arrant glib foolish nonsense and frippery. I would conclude my burble and babble, and watch him lean back to consider what I had said, and then after a moment he would say something quietly encouraging, and then often he would say several more encouraging things, and then he would finally gently comment on what it was I had said, but never with the slightest sneer or slice, though much of what I said surely deserved to be dismissed out of hand. There was a pace and a rhythm to his listening, it seems to me, such that the listening was far more important than anything else; in so many people the answering, the opinionating, the jockeying, the topping, the shouting of self, the obviation of the other, is the prime work in conversation, but this was not so for my dad, the best listener I have ever known.

His listening is now largely a thing of the past; he and his ears have achieved a great and venerable age, and his hearing is a shadow of what it once was. His mind is as sharp or even more so than it ever was; his generosity and grace remain oceanic; and you could search whole galaxies, to no avail, for a gentler, wittier man. But this morning I find that I very much miss that one little thing he did so well, that was not little—the way he stared at your face as you spoke, with all his soul open and alert for your story, and how he would wait a few beats when you were done, in case there was a coda coming, and then he would lean back and consider what you had just said, and then finally lean forward again and say something gentle and encouraging. That he would often then add something wise and piercing is true, but that is not what I want to leave you with; I want to celebrate his listening, for it is now nearly gone from this world, and it was a rare and extraordinary and unforgettable thing.

His Weirdness

A friend of mine is dying in the fast lane, he says, smiling at the image, for no man ever loved as much as he did zooming those long stretches of highway in the West, where there are no speed limits or curves or cops and nothing to kill you but sudden antelopes. But now he can see his exit up ahead, he says, and he has slowed down to enjoy the ride. He's been pondering the sparrows, who do not sow and neither do they reap, he says, shuffling into his yard armed with fistfuls of seed.

The woman who loves him watches him go, smiling. There are so very many tiny things that are exactly him and no other man on earth, she says: When he shaves his neck every other day he bangs his razor against the right side of the sink, and there's a little tiny scatter of hairs, which drives me stark raving insane, because never once in forty years has he remembered to rinse that off, despite one million promises to do exactly that. One time I wrote the words *Clean the sink!* actually *in* the sink, with a big red arrow pointing to the place where he bangs his razor, which made him laugh so hard I thought he was going to lose a kidney, which he didn't, nor did he clean the sink. Also he has a pair of boxers that are so incredibly ancient and threadbare you can, I kid you not, see through them. It's like eight threads with a waistband holding them together, but God forbid he throws them out. I have pointed out to him that this article of clothing is no longer serving the purpose for which it was designed, but he won't let them go, which tells you something about his commitment, or his craziness. Also he has a weird habit of slicing off the crust of a loaf of bread an inch at a time, which drives me stark raving insane, each piece the size of a quarter, which leaves a naked, crustless loaf of bread on the table, and who wants a loaf that looks like a skinned snake? Also even before he got sick, he shuffled, you know? He never lifts his feet. The kids and I always thought it was because he's distracted all the time. There are ten things going on in his head at once, and walking properly is just not on his priority list, walking is something he can do on autopilot. But it sounds like there's a rhinoceros in the hallway, and after you hear that ten thousand times, you want to shriek, *My god, will you walk like a normal person!* But he's not normal, you know. That's the point. Also he hums all the time, and he doesn't hear it. Every day a new set of songs. Lately it's all Beach Boys, all the time. He says he used to get in trouble in school when he was a kid because he would be humming during tests and exams and driving the other kids and the teacher stark raving insane. Same thing happened at work, he says: he would be in meetings with his soundtrack going full blast, and after a while he'd wonder why everybody was staring at him. I have been listening to his humming for forty years, and, me personally, I think Van Morrison is the all-time playlist champion, although there was a long stretch there, two or three years, where it was mostly West Coast jazz, Chet Baker and Art Pepper and stuff like that. See, that'll all be gone when he goes, and that's what makes me cry at night. Mostly we just try to enjoy the time we have left, but sometimes I think ahead to when the sink will be totally clean in the morning, and that will be awful, or the bread won't have white holes where he's cut off pieces of crust the size of a quarter. What kind of raving lunatic would do such a thing? Only him. People think what we'll miss most is his humor and kindness and all that, which we will, but lately I think what we'll miss the most is his weirdness. His weirdness is what he was. Everybody else saw him as a good guy, but we saw him as the humming rhinoceros in the hallway, you know what I mean? And sometimes I get really scared of waking up in the morning and not hearing that stupid shuffle. I hate that shuffle. I love that shuffle. That's as close as I can get to what I am trying to say.

Let's go feed the sparrows with him. You will not be surprised to hear that he has a weird thing going with feeding the birds: a different seed every week, and he keeps track of which ones they like. He has a piece of paper pinned up on the garage near the bird feeder with his charts on it and also, God help me, a section for comments from the birds, with a little tiny pencil. I told you the man was a total nut. Did you think I was kidding? I was not kidding. What kind of man would go to the trouble of making a pencil exactly two centimeters long? It works too. He tested it, of course. And it tells you something about him that, deep in his heart, he wouldn't be surprised if someday he shuffled out to feed the birds and found a tiny complaint written there. Nobody who ever lived would be happier to find a complaint from the sparrows about the seed of the week, believe me. He'll probably write a little tiny reply from the management, you know? With a promise to do better.

The Tender Next Minute

One time when we were kids my two younger brothers
And I were absorbed with ropes and climbing and what
Heights could be scaled by intrepid adventurers like us,
And we scaled the garage, and then we scaled a massive
Sweet gum, and then we tried to scale a neighbor's shed
But he glared and roared and we escaped into the hedge
Riven with tunnels and lairs that only we knew, and it's
That moment in the lurk of the hedge that I want to sing
Here for a moment. We huddled, panting, at the second
Turn, under the iglooish canopy of the forsythia bushes.
I had the rope, and my next brother had our kid brother,
Actually holding him by the hand, and we were smiling
And thrilled and frightened and sunlight rippled through
The tiny yellow flowers of the bushes and not far away
A robin inquired as to just what was all this hullabaloo?
You were there too, remember, in *your* childhood cave,
The moist soil, the laboring beetles, the unwritten poem
Of the lost leaves, the duff, the thin spidery bones of old
Twigs. Once in a while we all stopped sprinting and just
Stared at what was there all around us, the wealth of dirt,
The sudden green feather about to adorn its second wild
Animal, the tender next minute waiting for us to emerge.

.

His Holiness the Dalai Lama,[*] Manifestation of Chenrezig, Bodhisattva of Compassion, Stops the Car Along the Road to Watch Children Play Soccer

And remembers playing soccer himself long ago,
In Taktser, or Roaring Tiger, in northeast Tibet,
Or what used to be Tibet, he thinks darkly, but he is
Too tired to be exhausted, and too used to laughter
To sink into a sometimes-very-welcome-despond,

---

[*] In May of 2013, His Holiness the Dalai Lama visited the University of Portland. As a security team inspected an incoming crowd of five thousand, U.P.'s Brian Doyle was enjoying the quiet in an anteroom lined with cases full of athletic trophies. A Tibetan monk wandered in. Drawn to the trophies, he asked BD, "What have these men and women done to merit golden shrines?" BD explained that they were athletes, the monk and writer discovered a shared love of sports, and within seconds they began arguing over whether soccer or basketball is the superior game. Though BD was delighted by the monk's resounding laugh, hoop is hoop and Brian is Brian: when the monk remained hoop-proof, BD tossed a word at him. Comparing four accounts of this moment, two of them Brian's own, there was controversy over whether the word was "pal," as in *Hey listen, pal!*, or "bub," as in *Hold on there, bub!* But there is no controversy over the fact that, soon after he hurled the word, an entourage of monks and secret service filed in, the monks reverently encircled BD's antagonist, and Brian realized he'd been hammering like a barroom sports junkie on the most revered spiritual figure of our time. The aftermath of the debate was positive for both men. Having been buried in honorific titles since early childhood, His Holiness seemed delighted to be a "pal" or "bub" long enough to be hammered on over sports. And Brian was so moved by the depth of the compassion hero's love for soccer that he opened up his capacious imagination, and the following Tibetan folk tale was born.

And too interested in the game to miss the moment
Unfolding as a lean lanky girl breaks from the pack

And bears down on the goalkeeper and fakes once
Twice and then lashes a howling shot to the upper
Right corner and the goalie leaps and flails and
The shot just misses and His Holiness clambers out
Of the car to applaud both the shot and the near-save.
The children turn to see who is clapping but he's no
One they know and no one's dad so they ignore him.

He leans against the warm flank of the car. The driver
Gets out too and lights a cigarette. The game resumes.
Neither man speaks for a moment. The sun is warm.
One day four men came to visit, says His Holiness.
I was asked to choose between two rosaries. I did so.
Then I was asked to choose between pairs of eyeglasses.
I was asked to choose a staff. I did these things. Then

They asked my parents if they might search my body
For the eight holy marks. When they were finished
Examining me they conferred among themselves.
Out behind our house my friends were playing soccer.
They were calling for me to come and play the game.
Lhamo! they called, Lhamo! The men were solemn.
They bowed to my father and my mother, and one man,

The oldest of them, said, We have found Avalokitesvara.
Lhamo! my friends kept calling. Bring your fast feet!
He is Tenzin Gyatso, the Ocean of Wisdom, said the man.
Also bring your ball because Sonam the idiot lost his ball!
He is Yeshe Norbu, the Wish-Fulfilling Gem, said the man.
Lhamo! If you do not come soon you have to be goalkeeper!
He is Jetsun Ngawang, the Holy Compassionate One,

Said the man, and he made a sign and everyone knelt,
Even my father and mother. For a moment no one spoke,
So I figured they were done with the matter at hand,
And I smiled to think of the game to come, because my
Ball loved the goal, but then the man said, He is Kundun,
The Presence, and everything was different ever after.

Two on Two

Once upon a time, a long time ago, I rambled through thickets of brawny power forwards and quicksilver cocksure guards and rooted ancient centers, trying to slide smoothly to the hoop, trying to find space in the crowd to get off my shot, trying to maneuver at high speed with the ball around corners and hips and sudden angry elbows, the elbows of twenty years of men in grade school high school college the park the playground the men's league the noon league the summer league, men as high as the seven-foot center I met violently during a summer-league game, men as able as the college and professional players I was hammered by in playgrounds, men as fierce as the fellow who once took off his sweats and laid his shotgun down by his cap before he trotted onto the court.

I got hurt, as most everyone does eventually; I got hurt enough to quit; back pains then back surgery then more surgeries; it was quit or walk, now I walk.

The game receded, fell away, a part of me sliding into the dark like a rocket stage no longer part of the mission. Now I am married and here come my children: my lovely dark-haired thoughtful daughter and three years later my squirming twin electric sons, and now my daughter is four and my sons are one each, and yesterday my daughter and I played two on two against my sons on the lovely burnished oak floor of our dining room, the boys who just learned to walk staggering like drunken sailors and falling at the slightest touch, my daughter loud lanky in her orange socks sliding from place to place without benefit of a dribble but there is no referee, only me on

236

my knees, dribbling behind my back and trick-dribbling through the plump legs of the boys, their diapers sagging, daughter shrieking with glee, boys confused and excited, and I am weeping weeping weeping in love with my perfect magic children, with the feel of the bright-red plastic tiny ball spinning in my hands, my arms at home in the old motions, my head and shoulders snapping fakes on the boys, who laugh; I lean long for a loose ball near the dining room table and shuffle so slowly so slowly on my knees toward the toy basket a mile, a hundred miles, eight feet away, my children brushing against my thighs and shoulders like dreams like birds; Joe staggers toward me, reaches for the ball, I wrap it around my back to my left hand, which picks up rapid dribble, Joe loses balance and grabs my hair, Lily slides by suddenly and cuts Joe cleanly away, taking a couple of hairs with him as he and Lily disappear in a tangle of limbs and laughs, a terrific moving pick, I would stop to admire it but here comes big Liam, lumbering along toward the ball as alluring and bright as the sun; crossover dribble back to my right hand, Liam drops like a stone, spins on his bottom to stay with the play, I palm the ball, show-fake and lean into a short fallaway from four feet away, ball hits rim of basket, bounces straight up in the air, Lily slides back into picture and grabs my right hand but I lean east and with the left hand catch and slam the ball into the basket all in one motion; and it bounces off a purple plastic duck and rolls away again under the table, and I lie there on the floor as Joe yanks at my left sock, and Lily sits on my chest, and Liam ever so gently so meticulously so daintily takes off my glasses, and I am happier than I have ever been.

What Were Once Pebbles
Are Now Cliffs

I am standing in the middle pew, far left side, at Mass. We choose this pew when possible for the light pouring and puddling through the stained-glass windows. The late-morning Mass is best because the sun finally made it over the castlements of the vast hospital up the hill and the sun has a direct irresistible shot at the windows and as my twin sons used to say the sun *loooves* jumping through the windows and does so with the headlong pleasure of a child.

They used to be small enough to choose different sun-shot colors on the floor and jump from one color to another, my sons. They would do this before Mass and after Mass and occasionally during Mass on the way back from being blessed by Father John in the years before their own First Communions. Sometimes they would rustle and fidget impatiently in the pews, and fiddle with missals, and fold the parish newsletter into ships and trumpets, and bang the kneeler up and down, until they were arrested by the wither of the maternal glare, but then came Communion, which meant Father John bending down from his great height like a tree in a storm and blessing them with his hand as big as a hat on their heads. They loved that, and loved whispering loudly *Hi Johnny!* to him, which would make him grin, which they counted as a win, to make the sturdy dignified celebrant grin like a kid right in the middle of Communion!

When they were three and four years old they used to stand on the pew next to me and lean on me as if I was a tree and they were birds. Sometimes one would fall asleep and I would sense this through my arm and shoulder so that when I sat down I would be sure to haul the sleeper down safely. Sometimes they would lean hard against me to try to make me grin like Father John grinned during Communion. Once I discovered that they had conspired before Mass to lean on Dad so hard that they would *squish Dad!* and he would get six inches taller *right there in the church!,* wouldn't that be funny? Sometimes they would lean against me just from a sheer simple mammalian affection, the wordless pleasure of leaning against someone you love and trust. But always I was bigger and they were smaller, then.

Then came years during which there was no leaning because generally they were leaning away from their parents and from the church and from authority in all its figments and forms and constitutions, and generally they sat silent and surly and solitary, even during the Sign of Peace, which distressed their parents, which was the point.

But now they are twenty and one is much taller than me and the other is much more muscular. One is lanky and one is sinewy. One is willowy and the other is burly. And the other day in Mass I leaned against one and then the other and I was moved, touched, pierced down to the fundaments of my soul. What were once pebbles are now cliffs. They are tall and strong and stalwart and charming and at the Sign of Peace people in all directions reach for them smiling. When I lean against them they do not budge and now I am the one leaning against men whom I love and trust and admire. Sometimes I lean too hard against them on purpose just to make them grin. Sometimes by chance I am the first one back from Communion and I watch as they approach, wading gracefully through the shivered colors of the sun streaming through the windows. Time stutters and reverses and it is always yesterday and today. Maybe the greatest miracle is memory. Think about that this morning, quietly, as you watch the world flitter and tremble and beam.

Last Prayer

Dear Coherent Mercy: Thanks. Best life ever.

Personally I never thought a cool woman would come close to understanding me, let alone understanding me but liking me anyway, but that happened!

And You and I both remember that doctor in Boston saying polite but businesslike that we would not have children but then came three children fast and furious!

And no man ever had better friends, and no man ever had a happier childhood and wilder brothers and a sweeter sister, and I was that rare guy who not only loved but liked his parents and loved sitting and drinking tea and listening to them!

And You let me write some books that weren't half bad, and I got to have a career that actually no kidding helped some kids wake up to their best selves, and no one ever laughed more at the ocean of hilarious things in this world, or gaped more in astonishment at the wealth of miracles everywhere every moment.

I could complain a little here about the long years of back pain and the occasional awful heartbreak, but Lord, those things were infinitesimal against the slather of gifts You gave mere me, a muddle of a man, so often selfish and small. But no man was ever more grateful for Your profligate generosity, and here at the very end, here in my last lines, I close my eyes and weep with joy that I was alive, and blessed beyond measure, and might well be headed back home to the incomprehensible Love from which I came, mewling, many years ago.

But hey, listen, can I ask one last favor? If I am sent back for another life, can I meet my lovely bride again? In whatever form? Could we be hawks, or otters maybe? And can we have the same kids again if possible? And if I get one friend again, can I have my buddy Pete? He was a huge guy in this life—make him the biggest otter ever and I'll know him right away, okay?

Thanks, Boss. Thanks from the bottom of my heart. See You soon.

Remember—otters. Otters rule. And so: amen.

Acknowledgments

To you, dear readers,

This extraordinary book your hands hold was made of more than paper and ink. It was made of admiration, altruism, awe, diligence, extension, generosity. It is a promise and a prayer. It is living proof that we are wise to hold compassion as our Lodestar and to believe that energy never ever is lost and that Brian James Patrick Doyle stirred up so much love in this world that his companions gave of themselves to gather his far-flung brilliant essays from the corners of the world and tuck them in between these covers so you might now know him more as we do, with his capacious humble heart, his soaring spirited stupendous mind, his tender copious humor, his feisty unfailing faith. Of course he had his foibles, was impossible to argue with, hummed through operas and meetings, was fond of repetition and being earlier than early at airports, but it was because of his relationship with time. He was attentive to and creative with it. He didn't hurry or worry it either. He charmed it. His greatest joy was using his to delight you. I believe Brian had already been to heaven and back and found it irresistible not to return and restore astonishment, which is a sacrament, which is what you have just received.

To you, Brian James Patrick, for asking me to make us.

To Lily Marie, Joseph James, and Liam Robert for being muses and music for your father's tall tales made with cinnamon and love. Each of you know how you have risen and grown and given. You are fortitude filled with life force.

To Ringo for teaching Brian what it means to love a house wolf.

To Kathleen Joan Yale for searching, typing, reading, typing, spread-sheeting, typing, permissioning, typing, all while winning the Gold

Nautilus Award for *Howl Like a Wolf!* with Atticus on your lap and Rosario on your back, and to Vin, coming in from fieldwork so the two of you could juggle one more layer of literary largesse squeezed somewhere between dinner, bedtime stories, and elusive slumber.

To H. Emerson Blake, Mr. Chip, for enlarging the *Orion* offices to hold all of Brian's essays till you can publish daily and for mastering dexterity in negotiating the negotiations of publishers, agents, editors, and innocents, for patient panache connecting all the professional threads while keeping the stunning magazine afloat, along with your bright boy Jay.

To David James Duncan for the dear, deep, witty foreword catching the hymn of him and for hearing the rhythm of Brian's music and choreographing the harmony all while not working on your own mammoth novel and not wandering your own mountains and rivers, and to Adrian, Celia, Ellie, and your two horses, two goats, two dogs, and covey of half-pint chickens.

To Paul Lucas for agenting and fetching Little, Brown and for guiding the humble through the publishing wheel.

To Ben George for editing by not editing Brian and for securing our perfect title. To Michael Steger, for courteous contracting tenacity.

To all of the above for enthusiasm and conviction.

To Fred Courtright for enduringly navigating the rights and retributions and fielding questions at all hours while moving to Florida.

To Kim and Perrin Stafford for guiding us to Fred Courtright and for your seasoned savory wisdom and countless roast chicken dinners.

To Thomas Booth for vigor and brio while answering mounds of queries and for publishing *Mink River* in the first place and to Meg B. Holden for pies.

To Chris and Jeananne Doherty for legal and other advice while moving to the twenty-sixth floor with a broken elevator and for thirty-three years of salmon feasts in Neskowin.

To Robert Miller Senior and Susan Richardson Miller for legal advice and general guidance and the best barbecued steaks in Damascus, not to mention Thanksgivings.

Acknowledgments

To Elisabeth Mary Miller for being Beth.

To all the optimistic, stellar, brave publishers and editors who gave first light to Brian's essays and graciously gave permission for them to be included in this collection. A special bow to Bernadette Walters and Martin Flanagan for imaging One Day Hill into being and for the hummingbird on the cover of *Thirsty for the Joy.*

To the long-legged, lovely, fiery Irish Ethel Clancy Doyle for mothering, teaching, tending, and for dusting the mountains and miles of bookshelves living and breathing in your home, feeding Brian's hungry mind with dreams and visions all the while. For birthing Kevin, Betsy, Peter, and Thomas to sandwich Brian in between instead of becoming a U.S. senator, and for marrying the erudite, dignified, and devilishly handsome James Aloysis Doyle, who fathered the lot of them, all of you gathering and laughing and arguing each evening at the dinner table, elbowing and jostling and elevating each other.

To James Aloysis Doyle, for all the hours in the wars and on the train to the city, keeping all of us and the *Catholic Press* alive and well and putting up storm windows and listening and leveling and typing columns in the basement instead of writing all of your own novels, presenting Brian (while he pondered going to the state college to play basketball or Notre Dame to pursue an English degree) with the infamous observation that you hadn't seen a lot of under-six-foot guys with ponytails and glasses in the NBA.

For the seventy-five years of your vibrant and desirous marriage, in sickness and in health, with the *Times* and tea, and for the incredible way you, our beloved Nana and Bopa, LIVE your buoyant faith, selflessly, nonjudgmentally, and sui generis-ly, which qualities marinated and flourished in the son you love so and sent out with stamps and a silver tongue.

To Kevin for being a hero to B. and for keeping Heron Hawk Eagle Egret Osprey company with him now.

To Depa for giving your brother his learning curves in music and rhythm and for your calm joy and peace and saffron and maroon socks hanging along the Hudson River.

To Peter for accompanying your brother through the oceans and

245

backroads and forests and bars of your brotherhood and for all the beauty you bring out of wood.

To Thomas for being the solid, sturdy, sumptuous son, and bait for your brothers. For always caring for others before your deep-sea dives or your golf games, all while raising funds to nourish young-adult minds.

To Jane, Sharon, Diane, Neal, Meghan, Jess, Jack, Henry, Conor, Rachel, Tara, Colleen for millions of easy connective bumping hours of laughing stories and stimulus in Merrick, Ireland, and Florida.

To Steve, Gregg, Susie, Bobby, George, Chris, Luke, Maddie, Catie, Tim, Ingrid, Mark, Susan, Maggie, Will, Sam, Katie, Brock, Samuel, Robert, Kesa, Tyrell, Leo, Maurice, Hannah, Mary, Erich, Lucas, Charlotte, John, Paula, Vincent, Grace, Michael for millions of easy connective bumping hours of laughing stories and stimulus in Neskowin, Portland, and Damascus.

To our dear friends on the court and off, in pubs, bookstores, libraries, classrooms, and campuses, at concerts, coffee shops, and chapels, at weddings and wakes, in kitchens and gardens and vine-yards, around your tables, on islands, highways, skyways, streets, and country roads, you know who you are and what you mean to us.

As Brian wrote for his friend the Reverend Bill Harper, "If a man cannot begin to count the oceans of love slathered in his personal direction, then he is rich far beyond calculation." Remember to be rich when fear comes.

If we are united, then there is no room for fear. Just miles and oceans and streams and rivers of long songs of gratitude.

Gratias vobis ago.

Mary Miller Doyle, July 22, 2019

appeared in *The Oregonian*. "Jones Beach" appeared in *Ecotone*, "Mea Culpa" in *Brevity*, and "The Final Frontier" and "Because It's Hard" (originally titled "A Monk Would Know Better") were published in *Sojourners*. "Yes" appeared in *Harper's* and the *Georgia Review*, and "The Wonder of the Look on Her Face" and "Two on Two" were published in *Creative Nonfiction*.

About the Author

Brian Doyle (1956–2017) was born in New York and attended the University of Notre Dame. He worked at *U.S. Catholic Magazine, Boston College Magazine,* and, up until his death, was the editor of *Portland* Magazine. He wrote a number of novels and works of nonfiction, and his essays appeared in the *New York Times, Atlantic Monthly, Harper's, Orion, American Scholar, America Magazine, The Sun,* and many more. He won the American Academy of Arts and Letters Award in Literature, the 2017 John Burroughs Medal for Distinguished Nature Writing, the Oregon Book Award, three Push-cart Prizes, among others, and had multiple essays included in *Best American Essays.*